SMALL-SCALE EVALUATION

SMALL-SCALE EVALUATION
Principles and Practice

Colin Robson

SAGE Publications
London • Thousand Oaks • New Delhi

ISBN 0-7619-5509-7 (hbk)
ISBN 0-7619-5510-0 (pbk)

SAGE Publications Ltd
1 Oliver's Yard
55 City Road
London EC1Y 1SP

SAGE Publications Inc
2455 Teller Road
Thousand Oaks
California 91320

SAGE Publications India Pvt. Ltd
B-42 Panchsheel Enclave
PO Box 4109
New Delhi 110 017

British Library Cataloguing in Publication data
A catalogue record for this book is available from the British Library

Printed on paper from sustainable sources

Typeset by Anneset, Weston-super-Mare, Somerset
Printed digitally and bound in Great Britain by
Lightning Source UK Ltd., Milton Keynes, Bedfordshire

To Joe, Sophie, Rose,
Alex and Tom

CONTENTS

PREFACE

Much of the literature on evaluation is written for professional evaluators, or for those who aspire to join their ranks. The conduct of evaluations is a relatively new area of expertise which is by no means fully professionalized. This text seeks to provide support and assistance to anyone involved in evaluations whether or not they have a professional background in the field. Relatively little has been published previously about the particular issues raised in carrying out small-scale, local, evaluations and it is hoped this focus will be of interest to those with an evaluation background when asked to carry out such a study. Those without previous experience in evaluating tend to get involved in small-scale evaluations and a major aim of the book is to help, and give confidence to, such persons.

A note on gender and language. In order to avoid the suggestion that all evaluators and others involved are males (or females) and the clumsy 'she/he', I use the plural 'they' whenever feasible. If the singular is difficult to avoid I use a fairly random sequence of 'she' and 'he'.

Colin Robson

ACKNOWLEDGEMENTS

Grateful thanks to the many colleagues I have worked with since the mid-seventies on a range of evaluations and related applied projects mainly carried out in partnership between the then Huddersfield Polytechnic and the Hester Adrian Research Centre, University of Manchester, particularly Judy Sebba, Peter Mittler and Chris Kiernan. Also to colleagues and students involved with the postgraduate programme in Social Research and Evaluation at the University of Huddersfield, the development, running and teaching of which contributed greatly to my education in things evaluative.

More recently I have managed to leave administrative duties behind and have concentrated on the highly rewarding task of supervising research students in a fascinatingly wide set of evaluative studies ranging from studies of services for children in need, through approaches to the teaching of high-ability students of the piano, to reducing the effects of low back pain in a biscuit factory. Particular thanks to colleagues Judith Milner, Wendy Parkin, Nigel Parton, George Pratt, Grant Roberts and Penny Wolff, and to students (and ex-students) Ros Day, Lorraine Green, Sally Johnson, Marian MacDonald, Roland Perrson, Nick Sutcliffe and Tara Symonds.

Thanks are also due to Mansoor Kazi, Director of the Centre for Evaluation Studies, University of Huddersfield, an enthusiastic proponent of the virtues of single-case methodology, and more recently scientific realism, in the evaluation of social work practice, for his infectiously energetic efforts on behalf of evaluation; and to Joe Wilson, Manager of Kirklees Education Social Work Service and his DfEE-funded team working on school attendance who have provided him with an invaluable test-bed for new approaches to evaluation from which I have profited indirectly. Particular thanks, as ever, to my wife Pat Robson for her help in turning the text into something closer to standard English, including gently pointing out where my Yorkshire linguistic roots were showing through.

In acknowledging my obvious intellectual debt to many who have gone before in developing the field of evaluation I would like to pay particular tribute to the work of Carol Weiss. She provided one of the earliest texts in the field (Weiss, 1972) and her second edition of the book (Weiss, 1998) maps the progress made in over a quarter of a century with a rare combination of wisdom, academic rigour and practicality. Anyone

wishing to make a serious study of evaluation after the introduction provided in this text should devour it. The reader will also note the influence of Ray Pawson and Nick Tilley and their provocative and
stimulating 'Realistic Evaluation'. My subsequent involvement with very
different groups of practitioners in workshop settings confirmed an
impression that the terminology of mechanisms, contexts and outcomes
derived from scientific realism, while initially somewhat daunting, provides a helpful framework for understanding what is going on in their
services and interventions. It has given me the confidence to introduce a
discussion of the value of this approach in the many evaluations which
seek to improve the service, program or whatever is being evaluated.

Thanks to colleagues on the Internet listerv EVALTALK, in particular
Sally Dittloff of the University of Nevada, who helped me trace the source
of the quotation from Kurt Lewin on p. 69. I also wish to give formal
acknowledgement of permissions given to reprint the following mater-
ial. To Falmer Press (Table 2.1, from King, 1995, Table 6.1, p. 88 © Falmer
Press). To Barnardo's (Figure 3.3, from Alderson, 1996, Section 3 'Privacy
and Confidentiality', pp. 107–8 © Barnardo's). To Sage Publications Inc.
(Appendix C, from Joint Committee on Standards, 1994, *Program
Evaluation Standards*, 2nd edn. © Sage Publications Inc., Table 3.1, from
Sieber, 1998, Table 5.1, p. 150 © Sage Publications Inc., Table 4.1 from
Herman *et al.*, 1987, Table 2, p. 27 © Sage Publications Inc., Figure 5.2,
from Fowler, 1998, pp. 365–6 © Sage Publications Inc., Table 6.2, from
Pawson and Tilley, 1997, Table 4.7, p. 112 © Sage Publications Inc.). To
Sally Johnson for the examples of a diary and an interview schedule
appearing as Figures 5.5 and 5.6 (Johnson, 1997, pp. 356–9 and 347–8,
respectively).

INTRODUCTION

Who is the Book for?

Anyone involved in commissioning, designing, carrying out or using small-scale evaluations of innovations, interventions, projects, services or programmes which focus on people. This includes policy-makers, managers, practitioners, service providers and users, as well as researchers, consultants and evaluators. It seeks to address the issues involved in mounting small-scale evaluations in fields such as health, social work and social policy, crime, education, business and management.

The direct audience is the person who is acting as an evaluator. I say 'acting as an evaluator' as many of those who I have in mind may not think of themselves as evaluators as such. They are acting as an evaluator because they have been asked to do so, possibly for the first time. The hope and intention of this book is that it will help such a person to carry out a worthwhile small-scale evaluation. Obviously experience does help, and it may be that the text will be of most value to those who have had one or two previous attempts at carrying out an evaluation. As a result of that experience you will appreciate some of the likely problems and complexities, and perhaps want to make a better job of it next time.

The book is intended to be reasonably self-sufficient. It should be feasible for someone to go through it and, even without previous evaluation experience, design and carry out a simple evaluation. References are provided for those who wish to delve deeper. In a small book like this it is not possible to do more than just scratch the surface of many complex issues which surround the field, particularly technicalities associated with the use of social science research methods and the statistical analysis of data. However, while the use of sophisticated research methodology will give you kudos in academic communities, and will be likely to improve the quality of your evaluation, it is by no means an essential feature of a worthwhile small-scale evaluation.

In my experience, the people most likely to be asked to carry out a small evaluation are either those with a previous background in social science research, or practitioners with some form of professional training. Both types of background are undoubtedly valuable for anyone asked to do an evaluation. However, an early warning might be in order that those familiar with relatively 'pure' approaches and the seductive certainties of experimental method may find adaptation to the realities of doing evaluations disturbing.

If you lack a social science background, do not despair. Common-sense and integrity, together with an appreciation of the major issues and decisions to be faced when evaluating, can carry you a long way. You provide the first two, and it is my job to help with the rest.

Policy-makers, administrators, practitioners and others will, I hope, gain an appreciation of the many different forms an evaluation can take and some understanding of what they might expect both from the evaluation and the evaluator. This may help to avoid the frustrating experience for an evaluator of the sponsor, or some other person with the power of specifying the nature of the evaluation, calling for, say, a survey when it is clear this approach is unlikely to answer the questions of interest to the sponsor. It should also make clear that sponsors, policy-makers, administrators, practitioners and others with an interest in the evaluation can have an active involvement in an evaluation. Indeed, that it is likely to be a more effective and useful study if they do.

What do you Need to be Able to Carry out an Evaluation?

This depends on the nature of the particular evaluation. Some may call for specific expertise in the use of a particular method of investigation such as running focus groups. Others may need facility with a computer package for statistical analysis. If you do not have the necessary skills to do this then there are two possibilities. You can review what is proposed, and cut it down to something you can handle. Or it may be possible to get others to do such things for you, providing you know what is required. It is worth stressing you are highly unlikely to be able to carry out any evaluation just using your own resources. One very valuable skill is that of persuading others to participate. Usually there will be people around who can not only add to the resources available, but also by their very involvement make it both a more enjoyable experience and a more useful evaluation.

Such personal and social skills, which also include sensitivity and tact, are of great importance when carrying out an evaluation. The need for integrity has already been stressed. You can get into very murky waters when evaluating and evaluations almost inevitably get you into ethical dilemmas and political power struggles. In such situations what you are going to need is a commitment to open-minded striving for 'truth'.

The 'scare-quotes' around the word indicate fundamental difficulties with such a concept as truth in the context of an evaluation, and the point can, perhaps, be best made negatively. An evaluator is not in the business of selling the product or the program. Your task is to seek to tell it as it is. It is not a polemical exercise where, by emotive language and selective use of information, you present a persuasive picture. There is, of course, a place for such strategies in the real world. And, it could be argued, that following a positive evaluation of a program, service or whatever, it would be remiss not to use marketing and promotional skills to further its dissemination and use. (Although this, in itself, is a slippery slope, and any attempts to sell on a false prospectus could well be counterproductive in the longer term.) The sin is to present something else as an honest evaluation. Forgive the sermon but there may well be pressures to paint the picture your sponsor wishes to see, and you should be forewarned about this.

What is a Small-Scale Evaluation?

To evaluate is to assess the worth or value of something. The 'somethings' which form the focus of the evaluations referred to in this book can be very varied. Typically there is some kind of program (or 'programme' in British English), innovation, intervention or service involving people which is being looked at. Commonly the intention is to help these people in some way. The nature of evaluation is considered in greater detail in the following chapter.

The focus in this book is the small-scale evaluation. The likely parameters of such evaluations are that they

- are *local* – rather than regional or national;
- involve a *single evaluator* – or possibly a small team of two or three;
- occupy a *short timescale* – perhaps completed in something between one month and six months;
- have to be run on *limited resources*; and
- take place at a *single site* – or possibly a small number of related sites.

Many small-scale evaluations are carried out by persons who already have a role within the organization where the evaluation is taking place. These are known as *'insider' evaluations*. The existing role can actually be as an evaluator, possibly combined with other roles, or something else entirely. Both 'outsider' and 'insider' evaluations, and the different issues involved in carrying them out, are covered in the book.

Using the Book

You will get most out of this book if you are in the situation of having to carry out a specific evaluation. Perhaps you

- have been asked to do this by your boss;
- and a small group of colleagues think some aspect of your practice should be the focus of an evaluation (and have managed to persuade the powers-that-be this would be a good idea);
- have carried out some mini-evaluation and enjoyed it; you have put in a successful bid to do something rather more substantial; or
- have to do a small evaluation as an assignment on a course.

Whatever route you have taken, the grounding of your thinking about evaluation in the realities of your own situation will focus your mind more than somewhat.

Even if you are not in the fortunate, if frightening, position of having an actual evaluation pending, my strong advice is to proceed as if you had. In other words, look around you and consider what might be the focus of a small-scale evaluation. This is, superficially, a simpler task than that of having a real project. You have a variety of choices limited only by your own imagination. The problem is in keeping this kind of virtual evaluation 'honest'. For it to be a useful learning exercise you will need to set strict and realistic limits on what is feasible in terms of the time and other resources you are likely to have available. However, providing you carry out the various exercises in the text in this spirit, you should profit. It is not unknown for virtual evaluations like this to turn into real ones when colleagues, and others whom you discuss it with, appreciate the potential value of an actual evaluation.

A Note on 'Tasks'

This Introduction and the chapters following are each followed by a set of 'tasks'. My recommendation is that you get the initial tasks started now, or at least as soon as practicable.

For the following chapters the suggestion is you first work your way through the whole of the book, noting the tasks and, perhaps, thinking how they might be approached but not actually completing them.

Then return to Chapter 1 and, working in 'real time' (i.e. the time dictated by the requirements of the evaluation and the people involved) go through the chapter tasks broadly in sequence. It may make sense to combine tasks for different chapters depending on how your meetings and contacts with those involved work out.

Initial Tasks

1. *Get an 'evaluation diary'*. This is a notebook in which you enter a variety of things relevant to the evaluation. It can take many different forms but an obvious one is an actual large-format diary with at least a page for each day (they come cheaply from about March each year!). An alternative is to have the equivalent of this on your computer. The kinds of things which might be entered include:

- Appointments made, and kept; together with an aide-mémoire of where you have put anything arising from the meeting (one strategy is to include everything here in the diary).
- Responses to the later tasks in the book. Any thoughts relevant to the evaluation, particularly when you decide to modify earlier intentions; reminders to yourself of things to be done, people to be chased up, etc.
- Taking stock of where you are; short interim reports of progress, problems and worries; suggestions for what might be done.

The diary can be invaluable when you get to the stage of putting together the findings of the evaluation and writing any reports. It acts as a brake on tendencies to rewrite history, and can in itself be a valuable learning device particularly when you cringe at early mistakes or, more positively, marvel at disasters avoided.

2. *Start using it.* In particular it will be useful to write down a short account of the evaluation you are hoping to do. Half a page, or so, will be long enough. It is best if you do this before reading further in the book, as it will then be possible for you to look at it later and, perhaps, gain some insights into the assumptions you are making about what evaluations can or should be. However, I obviously can't stop you from reading on and returning to the task.

1
EVALUATION: THE WHAT AND THE WHY

Consider a project which seeks to help single parents to get a job. Or one which aims to 'calm' traffic in a village and reduce accidents. Or an attempt to develop healthy eating habits in young school children through the use of drama in the classroom. Or an initiative trying to cut down shoplifting from a supermarket. Or a firm where management wants to make more efficient use of space and resources by providing bookable workstations for staff rather than dedicated offices. These situations are all candidates for being evaluated. Your own possible evaluation might be very different from any of these. Don't worry; the range of possibilities is virtually endless. Do bear your proposed evaluation in mind, and test out for yourself the relevance of the points made to it when reading through the chapter.

Evaluation is concerned with finding something out about such more or less well intentioned efforts as the ones listed above. Do obstacles in the road such as humps (known somewhat whimsically in Britain as 'sleeping policemen'), chicanes and other 'calming' devices actually reduce accidents? Do the children change the choices they make for school lunch? Are fewer rooms and less equipment needed when staff are deprived of their own personal space?

The answer to the first question about obstacles is likely to be more problematic than that to the other two. It calls for consideration of aspects such as where one collects data about accidents. Motorists might be dissuaded from travelling through the humped area, perhaps transferring speeding traffic and resulting accidents to a neighbouring district. Also, when are the data to be collected? There may be an initial honeymoon period with fewer or slower cars and a reduction in accidents. Then a return to pre-hump levels. The nature or severity of the accidents may change. With slower traffic there could still be the same number of accidents, but fewer of them would be serious in terms of injury or death. Or more cyclists might begin to use the route, and the proportion of accidents involving cyclists rise. Either way a simple comparison of accident rates becomes somewhat misleading.

In the study of children's eating habits, assessing possible changes at lunchtime appears reasonably straightforward. Similarly, in the third example, senior management could more or less guarantee that efficiency, assessed purely in terms of the rooms and equipment they provide, will be improved. However, complications of a different kind lurk here. Measures of numbers of rooms and amount of equipment may be the obvious way of assessing efficiency in resource terms, but it could well be that it was not appropriate or sensible to concentrate on resources when deciding whether or not this innovation was a 'good thing'. Suppose the displaced office workers are disenchanted when a different way of working is foisted upon them. Perhaps their motivation and productivity falls. It may be that turnover of staff increases; and profits fall overall notwithstanding the reduction in resource costs.

It appears that a little thought and consideration of what is involved reveal a whole host of complexities when trying to work out whether or not improvement has taken place. In the traffic 'calming' example the overall aim of reducing accidents is not being called into question. Complexities enter when deciding how to assess whether or not a reduction has taken place. With the children it might be argued that what is really of interest is what the children eat at home, which might call for a different kind of intervention where parents are also targeted. In the office restructuring example the notion of concentrating on more efficient use of resources is itself being queried.

Such complexities make evaluation a fascinating and challenging field calling for ingenuity and persistence. And because virtually all evaluations prove to be sensitive, with the potential for upsetting and disturbing those involved, you need to add foresight, sensitivity, tact and integrity to the list.

Why Evaluate?

The answers are very various. They range from the trivial and bureaucratic ('all courses must be evaluated') through more reputable concerns ('so that we can decide whether or not to introduce this throughout the county') to what many would consider the most important ('to improve the service'). There are also, unfortunately, more disreputable pretexts for evaluation ('to give me a justification for closing down this service'). This text seeks to provide help in the carrying out of evaluations for a range of reputable purposes. And to provide you with defences against being involved with the more disreputable ones.

Few people who work today in Britain or any other developed society can avoid evaluation. It is also high on the agenda of those seeking to help developing countries by means of aid programs; see, for example Selener (1997). There seems to be a requirement to monitor, review or appraise virtually all aspects of the functioning of organizations in both public and private sectors. Certainly, in the fields of education, health and social services with which I have been involved, practitioners and professionals complain, often bitterly, of the stresses and strains and increased work-load this involves. We live in an age of accountability; of concern for value for money. Attempts are made to stem ever-increasing budget demands by increasing efficiency, and by driving down the unit of resource available to run services. In a global economy, commercial, business and industrial organizations seek to improve their competitiveness by increasing their efficiency and doing more for less.

This book is written in part in the spirit of 'if you can't beat 'em, then join 'em'. It seems highly unlikely that the millennium will bring about any reduction in such activities, and hence there is likely to be gainful employment in the foreseeable future for those carrying out reviews, appraisals and evaluations. Currently an alarming amount of this activity is carried out by persons who have little knowledge about the task. They are, at best, often committed to an unthinking adoption of a particular view of what is involved in an evaluation. Some appreciation of the issues and complexities in evaluating might lead to more satisfactory and useful outcomes.

It is also written in the faith that there is a positive side to evaluation. A society where there is a serious attempt to evaluate its activities and innovations, to find out if and why they 'work', should serve its citizens better. The necessary knowledge and skills to carry out worthwhile evaluations are not beyond someone prepared to work through a text of this kind – although it will undoubtedly help to be able to consult someone with a specialist background in evaluation. As discussed in the next chapter, it is highly likely that your evaluation will be improved if you collaborate with others possessing different types of expertise. The book will help you to ask the right questions of such persons.

What is Evaluation?

Dictionary definitions refer to evaluation as assessing the value (or worth, or merit) of something. The 'something' focused on here is some kind of innovation, or intervention, or project, or service. It involves people in one or more ways. Perhaps as the providers of the service, or in setting up and running the intervention. Almost inevitably as participants in the innovation or project and as clients of the service.

It is, perhaps, most commonly referred to as *program evaluation*, where 'program' is a generic term referring to any of the activities covered above; and where the spelling betrays the largely North American origins of this particular specialism. However, my experience has been that using the term program evaluation narrows the concept unhelpfully with some audiences, and hence I will stick with evaluation and try to spread the examples around amongst innovations, interventions, projects, programs and services. Feel free to translate into whichever of these has most relevance – even to 'programmes' for any British English chauvinists.

Rather than listing 'innovations, interventions, projects, programs or programmes, and services' every time, and disliking the latinate 'evalu-and' I will mainly use program or, sometimes, service. Feel free to sub-stitute whatever makes most sense in your own situation.

There are many kinds of evaluation other than those which focus on programs or services for people, e.g. the evaluation of traffic 'calming' schemes discussed earlier or of computer software. While such evalua-tions may well require consideration of some aspects different from those covered in this text, many of the same principles apply. Similarly, those concerned with the evaluation of physical rather than 'people' services will find that many of the same issues arise – a point brought home to me recently when looking at a text on *Evaluation for Village Water Supply Planning* (Cairncross et al., 1980).

Evaluation and Research

The position taken here is that while the terms 'evaluation' and 'research' denote rather different territories, there can profitably be a considerable amount of overlap between them. A high-quality evaluation calls for a well thought-through design and the collection, analysis and interpreta-tion of data. Following the canons of social science research helps to ensure the trustworthiness of any findings and recommendations. This by no means restricts the practice of evaluation to those with background and training in such research, but it does mean those without it need advice and support. A text such as this should help, primarily in sensi-tising you to what you don't know, and hence to when you should either keep away from something or call for help.

One clear difference between research and evaluation is that the latter, if only through the derivation of the term, carries notions of assessing 'value' with it. Research on the other hand is traditionally seen as con-cerning itself with the rather different activities of description, explana-tion and understanding. There is now wide recognition that researchers themselves are not 'value-free' in their approach. However, the conven-tions and procedures of science provide checks and balances. Attempting to assess the worth or value of an enterprise is a somewhat novel and disturbing task for some researchers when they are asked to make the transition to becoming evaluators. As discussed in Chapter 3, evaluation also almost always has a political dimension (small and/or large P). Greene (1994, p. 531) emphasises that evaluation 'is integrally intertwined with political decision-making about societal priorities, resource alloca-tion, and power'. Relatively pure scientists, whether of the natural or social stripe, may find this aspect disturbing.

A distinction is sometimes made between evaluation and *evaluation research*. This, in part, reflects an often heated debate in evaluators' circles about whether evaluation is a separable activity from research; or a par-ticular kind of applied research; or whether it is sometimes research and sometimes not. This distinction turns on the breadth or narrowness of view of both evaluation and research that are adopted. It is obviously

Table 1.1 *Some purposes of evaluation: likely questions posed by sponsor or program staff*

To find out if client needs are met	To improve the program	To assess the outcomes of a program	To find out how a program is operating	To assess the efficiency of a program	To understand why a program works (or doesn't work)
What should be the focus of a new program? Are we reaching the target group? Is what we provide actually what they need?	How can we make the program better (e.g. in meeting needs; or in its effectiveness; or in its efficiency)?	Is the program effective (e.g. in reaching planned goals)? What happens to clients as a result of following the program? Is it worth continuing (or expanding)?	What actually happens during the program? Is it operating as planned?	How do the costs of running the program compare with the benefits it provides? Is it more (or less) efficient than other programs?	They are unlikely to seek answers to this – but such understanding may assist in improving the program and its effectiveness

Note: For 'program' read 'service'; or 'innovation'; or 'intervention'; (or 'programme'!) as appropriate.

possible to attempt an evaluation which would be unlikely to be considered research (for example 'evaluating' restaurants for a published guide). However, the kind of '... diligent investigation of a program's characteristics and merits' (Fink, 1995, p. 2) which is likely to lead to worthwhile information about its operation, sounds very much like a description of a particular kind of research. Providing, that is, we do not tie ourselves to a restrictive definition of research, such as one which only considers randomized control trials focusing on program goals to be admissible.

Possible Foci for Evaluation

Evaluation is a field with a short, hectic and somewhat chaotic history. An early (1960s) concentration on *experimental* and *quasi-experimental* (Campbell and Stanley, 1966) research designs was largely superseded by attempts to develop evaluations which could be more easily used in the actual process of decision-making. This was characterized by Weiss (1987) as a shift from a knowledge-driven to a use-led approach; and, influentially, by Patton (1978) as 'utilization-focused'. Later 'paradigm' wars between authors holding radically different views of the nature of evaluation eventually take us through to so-called 'fourth generation evaluation' (Guba and Lincoln, 1989) variously labelled as 'naturalistic' and 'constructivist'.

Currently there seems to be a trend towards pluralistic approaches, which seek to synthesize, or at least put together, what they see as the best aspects of specific models. Thus Rossi advocates 'comprehensive' evaluation (Rossi and Freeman, 1993), which in some ways recapitulates the call for breadth and depth in evaluation which was present in the work of one of the earliest evaluators, Lee J. Cronbach (1963).

This is not the place to attempt a full review of the various twists and turns in the development of evaluation methodology (see Shadish *et al.*, 1991, for a detailed account). Table 1.1 attempts to capture some of the approaches such a review reveals. The table does not provide an exhaustive list of possible purposes of evaluation. Nor is it intended to suggest that evaluations must, or should be, exclusively focused on just one of these goals. This topic is returned to in Chapter 4 which considers the implications of different approaches for the design of evaluations.

In some ways the purpose of 'improvement' of a program is rather different from the others. Generally, any improvement will concern changes in respect of one or more of the other purposes. It could be that client needs are met more adequately. Or that the outcomes are improved; or efficiency increased, etc. When a program is running it is rare to find that those involved are not interested in its improvement. Even with a well established and well regarded program it is difficult and probably unwise to accept it as perfection. More typically there will be substantial room for improvement, and an evaluation of a program with problems will be better received by those involved if improvement is at least one of the purposes. Indeed there are ethical and practical problems in calling for the co-operation of program staff if you can't claim, with honesty, there is something in it for them. Potential improvement of the program is a good incentive.

What do they Think they Want?

You should now have an initial idea of the kinds of purposes an evaluation might serve. It is quite likely the people who want to get the evaluation carried out have their own ideas about what it should concentrate on. These views might be informed by a knowledge of evaluation and its terminology, but not necessarily so.

Who are 'they', the 'people who want to get the evaluation carried out'? This varies considerably from one evaluation to another. A common terminology refers to 'sponsors'. That is a person (sometimes a group of people) with the responsibility for setting up and funding the evaluation. Your knowledge of the program or service, together with discussions with the sponsors, should help in getting a feeling for where they would like the emphasis to be. It is very likely that, even when there is a clearly expressed wish to concentrate on one area, they will wish to have some attention to the others. For example they may indicate the main thing is to find out whether their goals are being achieved, but say they are also interested in the extent to which the program is being delivered as originally planned.

An important dimension is whether you are dealing with an existing program or service, or something new. If the latter you may well find the sponsors are seeking help in deciding what this new thing might be – in other words they are looking for some kind of assessment of the presently unmet needs of potential clients. Perhaps they appreciate that current provision should be extended into new areas as situations, or responsibilities, or the context, change. This is not an evaluation of a program per se but of the need for a program.

With a currently running program or service, the main concern might still be whether needs are being met. Or it could shade into a more general concern for what is going on when the program is running. As indicated in Table 1.1 there are many possibilities. One of your initial tasks is to get out into the open not just what the sponsors think they need, but also what they will find most useful but have possibly not thought of for themselves. Sensitizing them to the wide range of possibilities can expand their horizons. Beware though of encouraging them to think all things are possible. Before finalizing the plan for the evaluation you are going to have to ensure it is feasible given the resources available. This may well call for a later sharpening of focus.

Understanding why a program works (or why it is ineffective) appears to be rarely considered a priority by sponsors, or others involved in the running and management of programs. Perhaps it smacks of the theoretical, only appropriate for pure research. However, I will be suggesting in Chapter 4 that devoting some time and effort to the 'why' question may pay dividends with eminently practical concerns such as improving the effectiveness of the program.

What are they Going to Find Credible?

Through discussions with the sponsors and others involved in the program or service to be evaluated, you will be beginning to clarify what it is they want to know. It is worth while at this early stage also to get a feel for the kind of information they are likely to find credible. Providing such information is likely to increase the chances that the findings will be used. Some audiences value what might be termed 'hard' data: numbers and statistics. For others, the telling quotation and circumstantial detail are what really communicate, whereas tables of quantitative data merely alienate them. What you find out about this will influence both the kind of evaluation design and the way in which reports are presented. It is possible to have more than one way of communicating the findings of the evaluation, which can be a means of dealing with different audiences.

Your own preferences and (probable) prejudices also come into this of course. However, while these, together with client preferences, will influence the general approach, the over-riding influence has to be the information that is needed to get the best possible answers to the evaluation questions.

It is also worth stressing that you have to be credible. You need to come over as knowing what you are doing. This is partly a question of perceived technical competence as an evaluator, where probably the best way of appearing competent is to be competent. Working with professionals and practitioners it will also help if you have a similar background to them. If they know you have been, say, a registered nurse for ten years then you have a lot in your favour with other nurses. The sensitive nature of almost all studies can mean that, particularly if there are negative findings, the messenger is the one who gets the blame. 'She might know something about evaluation but obviously doesn't understand what it's really like to work here' to neutralize the experienced evaluator; as against 'I'm not sure that someone with a practitioner background can distance themselves sufficiently to give an objective assessment' to deal with the experienced practitioner.

Chapter 1: Tasks

1.   From discussions with the sponsor(s) try to establish:

    a)   what they see as the main purpose, or purposes, of the evaluation; and

    b)   what are the questions they want the evaluation to answer.

It may be helpful to refer to Table 1.1.

2. Then try to find out how it is proposed to use the findings of the evaluation. If (as is not unknown) this has not yet been thought about (gently) point out there is not much point in commissioning an evaluation which is not going to be used in some way.

Note:
a) It isn't necessary to be very specific at this stage. Your main concern is to establish the kind of thing they are after.
b) Don't encourage huge long lists of evaluation questions. Try to get them to specify the central question, perhaps with others as subsidiary.
c) As discussed in the next chapter, there is much to be said for getting others involved in most aspects of an evaluation. Similarly, it will be very helpful if you can persuade others to take part in the tasks for this chapter and those in following chapters.

2
THE ADVANTAGES OF COLLABORATION

As an evaluator it is virtually impossible for you to do a good job by relying solely on your own resources. You need the co-operation of others, if only to gain access to people or to provide you with information. Traditional models of social science research call for passive co-operation rather than any more active form of collaboration. Similarly, early models of evaluation tended to follow the objective scientist style where those taking part were research 'subjects' and the objective was to acquire 'truth', in the form of reliable and valid data, from them. Barkdoll (1980) contrasts this evaluative style with a 'surveillance and compliance' style adopted by some evaluators which is much closer to the stance of auditors or detectives. The goal is justice and the rooting out of wrong-doing. A third style is consultative and co-operative, aiming to work together with practitioners and others in a joint search for information.

Patton (1982, p. 58), in describing Barkdoll's typology, makes the pragmatic point that, while each of the three approaches has clear strengths, if a major aim is the actual utilization of any evaluation findings, then both the scientist and the auditor/detective model have severe shortcomings. Discovering scientific truth does not in itself make it at all likely that findings are acted on. Securing the verdict and, say, establishing that there has been non-compliance, may provide crucial evidence to justify closure of a program and, in that sense, action on the findings, but doesn't necessarily facilitate more constructive utilization.

There are also likely effects on the actual process of the evaluation. Increasingly, potential research 'subjects' are hostile to the notion they are being used. While the scientist/evaluator may be getting something out of it in the form of consultancy fees and/or publications there are no obvious gains for them. It is not too difficult for subjects to find ways of sabotaging or subverting the evaluation if views of this kind take root. Equally, or greater, negative reactions to the evaluator viewed as an auditor or law enforcement officer are highly predictable.

You need the active involvement of all those involved in the program or service if you are to achieve a quality evaluation which has some chance of being both useful and used. It is pretty self-evident you are more likely to achieve this by taking consultation very seriously.

Stakeholders

Anyone who has a stake, or interest, in an evaluation (in the sense that they are involved in or affected by it) is a stakeholder. Potentially this could be a very wide audience, but the key players are typically:

- *Policy-makers and decision-makers*: those responsible for taking decisions about the setting up, continuation, closure, expansion of programs or services.
- *Sponsors*: organizations, groups or individuals responsible for setting up and/or funding programs or services and their evaluation.
- *Management*: those responsible for managing the programs or services.
- *Staff* or *practitioners*: persons responsible for its delivery (they are sometimes referred to as 'participants', but this typically refers to their participation in an evaluation).
- *Clients* or *participants*: persons targeted by or taking part in the program or service.
- *Evaluators*: those responsible for the design and/or conduct of the evaluation.
- *Interested others*: people, groups or organizations geographically, organizationally or politically 'close', e.g. nearby residents, local politicians, providers of possible competing programs or services.

Policy-makers and decision-makers. Clearly they are interested in getting assistance in their making of policy and the taking of decisions. Why should they use the evaluation to help with these tasks? They are only likely to do this if they consider the evaluation is focusing on issues they feel are important. And only if they have confidence in you as an evaluator to do a good job. Both aspects call for their active involvement in the development of the evaluation design when, it is hoped, they will be favourably impressed by your competence and sensitivity.

Sponsors. The extent to which the sponsors are, or wish to be, involved in the evaluation and its design will vary considerably from one evaluation to another. At one extreme you may be asked to work to a very tight brief, where you are effectively a 'hired hand' with all-important decisions about the evaluation having already been made. Whether you accept such a brief will depend on your perception of its adequacy and appropriateness. And, of course, how badly you need the job and the money. At the other extreme you could simply be asked to get on with it, probably within a specified budget. In such circumstances it is highly desirable you work with them to clarify their expectations in a manner similar to that described above with policy-makers (indeed, the policy-makers may also be the sponsors).

The sponsors, as sponsors, are unlikely to have direct responsibility for whether or not the findings of the evaluation are utilized although it would be sensible of them to build this aspiration into the evaluation brief. However, their evaluation of how you have done the job could well influence your chances of being supported for future evaluations.

Management. Involving management and taking note of what their interests are in relation to the evaluation are both of practical importance in the conduct of the evaluation and of future significance for implementation. Their literal and metaphorical 'opening of doors' for you can make all the difference. Where there are different levels of management it may be necessary to ensure all are involved. Just because the head teacher has had her say and promised active co-operation doesn't mean the deputy with responsibility for day-to-day running of the school is going to facilitate things for you if they have not been involved, particularly if they are sceptical about the evaluation.

Staff or *practitioners.* Sponsorship and management approval is necessary but not sufficient. You will also need some form of direct involvement from those responsible for carrying out the program or running the service. Their concerns and likely worries about the implications of the evaluation for themselves have to be addressed. Again, this is important both for the conduct of the evaluation and for possible future utilization of findings.

Clients or *participants.* It could be argued that the clients, those targeted by the program or service, have most at stake. However, there are often considerable difficulties in obtaining their 'voice'. They may be reluctant to give an opinion, fearing possible repercussions. For programs and services directed at the socially disadvantaged or those with learning difficulties, there may be communication problems. Notwithstanding such difficulties it may be crucial to get a good involvement from clients. For some evaluative purposes this will be a direct part of the evaluation itself.

An alternative or additional avenue to getting the participants' voice heard is via relevant associations or organizations; for example those acting for the homeless or disabled. In an industrial or business setting, union or staff representatives might fulfil this function.

Evaluators. The prime interest for the evaluator is in carrying out a good-quality evaluation which is then utilized. As pointed out in discussing the roles of the other stakeholders, this is only likely to come to pass when the other stakeholders have an active involvement and some kind of voice in the focus and design of the evaluation. There is a potential dilemma here. If the evaluator is the person with the background and experience in evaluation then it might be thought she should have the responsibility for its design and conduct to ensure it is of good quality. But if she does this by herself it is unlikely to carry the various stakeholders with it in a way that facilitates either whole-hearted co-operation with the process, or subsequent utilization.

There is no easy solution. Given that the involvement of key stakeholders seems essential, a way forward is for the evaluator effectively to train them to play a part in the evaluation. This does not mean they need to have mastery of the technical vocabulary of the field; you can do the translation. What is needed is for them to appreciate the range of possibilities for the evaluation and, perhaps most crucially, the need for an empirical orientation. What you are seeking to foster is a commitment to getting the best possible answers to what has been agreed as the key evaluation questions, within the constraints of the resources and time available.

A related practical point is that it is likely to be more efficient for this involvement to take place in a group setting. Working in this way not only avoids a whole series of bilateral meetings with different stakeholders, but also facilitates the making of decisions about the evaluation. There are problems. Group processes are complex, and running an effective group demands further skills on your part.

Remember that, even if you are successful in getting other stakeholders to dance to the evaluation drum, as several commentators have pointed out, evaluators must accept the fact their efforts are just one of many potential inputs influencing decisions and actions. Clear findings from an evaluation may be ignored, particularly if the decision indicated is a difficult one, or the action apparently against the decision-makers' interests.

Interested others. Ask yourself who else is likely to be interested in, or affected by, the evaluation and its findings. If the evaluation is of a program and there are, perhaps, two other programs with similar objectives in the area, then stakeholders in these other programs could have a legitimate interest in this evaluation. Focusing the evaluation in a way that permits comparisons between the programs is one option. A proposed service or facility in a neighbourhood giving 'care in the community' for persons with mental disorders might excite concerns from those living nearby. While there is an understandable tendency to keep such developments under wraps to avoid the NIMBY (Not In My Back Yard) response, an early and carefully planned involvement of local representatives might avoid intransigence. (Although it also puts on the agenda the choice of alternative sites.)

Stakeholder Evaluation

In practice the sponsors, management and staff are probably the stakeholders most likely to take a keen interest in the evaluation and its findings. The sponsors because they have paid for the evaluation; management and staff because they are the ones likely to be in some sense judged by the findings of the evaluation and have much at stake.

From the point of view of facilitating utilization, these key stakeholders should be actively involved in shaping and focusing the evaluation so that it links in with their interests and concerns. There is good research evidence from several different literatures (e.g. those on diffusion of innovation and the psychology of change) that 'people are more likely to accept and use information, and make changes based on information, when they are personally involved in and have a personal stake in the decision-making processes aimed at bringing about change' (Patton, 1982, p. 61). Patton also cites evidence from the empirical literature on evaluation and policy analysis showing that utilization of evaluation is enhanced by high-quality stakeholder involvement in, and commitment to, the evaluation process.

The bringing together of key stakeholders can have benefits over and above those connected with the current evaluation. As Huberman (1990) argues, the collaboration established during the evaluation, what he terms the 'linkages', may be more important. Given this has been a positive experience, it will be more likely that in the future whenever an appropriate situation arises, these links will be used. So schools, social services or whatever will not only be predisposed to think in evaluative terms when an issue or problem arises but they will also have a pre-existing network to facilitate that evaluation.

Other Models of Involvement

In a stakeholder evaluation, as many as possible of those with a stake in the evaluation make a contribution. However, even when practitioners are involved directly in a stakeholder evaluation, this still leaves the evaluator as the person ultimately in charge of the planning and execution of the evaluation. The role of the other stakeholders is advisory and consultative. Other models give a privileged position and more active role to staff, usually referred to as practitioners, as shown in Table 2.1.

Participatory Evaluation

This approach, while it still gives the major evaluative role to the evaluator, has practitioners taking a full role in carrying out the evaluation. Typically a small number of practitioners take responsibility for the day-to-day operation of the evaluation. Cousins and Earl (1995) provide a useful set of papers on participatory evaluation in an educational context, including both case studies and analyses of the model (see especially Huberman, 1995). As King (1995) notes, there have been several traditions of participatory research. John Dewey and his colleagues at the turn of the century involved both teachers and students in classroom inquiry. A central feature is the interchange of information between researcher and practitioner so that the latter takes the information on board and then bases future action upon it. Hence there are shared characteristics with 'action research', as discussed below.

In participatory evaluation there is a joint responsibility between evaluator and participants. Cousins and Earl (1992) argue that this jointness gives a necessary active role to participants while still helping to maintain the rigour which is also necessary. Huberman, while very sympathetic to these aspirations, raises several caveats. In part this is because of some ambiguity as to who is a 'participant'. If teachers in a school

Table 2.1 *Comparison of approaches to collaboration*

	Stakeholder	Participatory evaluation	Practitioner-centred action research
Who's in charge of the study?	Evaluator as principal investigator	Evaluator, with assistance of practitioner/student at first	Practitioners, with assistance of research consultants
What practitioners are involved in the study?	Large number of stakeholders; anyone with a stake in the program	Small number of primary users	Action researchers
How do practitioners participate?	Consultative role; give information on context, information needs	Active role; engage in 'nuts and bolts' of evaluation process	Active role; control the research process
What time frame?	Length of study	Length of study or ongoing	Ongoing research cycle; organizational learning
What involvement in theory development?	[If any] Develop program theory	Develop program theory (theories-in-action, mental models)	[If any] Develop practical theory or critical theory

Source: Adapted from King (1995, Table 6.1).

work with an evaluator on a project in their own school that is one thing. If administrators, local authority advisers or inspectors, or program co-ordinators are evaluating what happens in that school by, say, interviewing teachers or pupils then that is a very different situation. Even with good will and trust this is a very sensitive situation, particularly in the context of league tables comparing the performance of schools.

When the participants in the evaluation are 'in house' there are difficult issues around the ownership and feeding back of data and findings. An evaluator has the mandate to 'tell it as it is'. Participants facing colleagues may feel greater inhibitions. Suppose the data are negative, perhaps revealing things about a current program which will be distressing to some. Responses to such revelations may be hostile, perhaps querying the methods, the data themselves, or even the good faith of those reporting them. This is probably part of the price one has to pay, with such conflict being a necessary part of life in schools and other organizations. Again it is a part of the evaluator's task to help colleagues appreciate the inevitable sensitivity of being the focus of an evaluation; and to prepare them for such reactions.

Practitioner-Centred Action Research

Action research is typified by the twin goals of improvement and involvement. It is an approach to inquiry undertaken by participants in social situations in order to improve both their practices and their understanding of the practices (McTaggart, 1991).

Traditional action research has the researcher or evaluator in charge of the study, although it is common to have support and assistance from practitioners. The main difference between action research and other forms of research is that, as the term suggests, it has an action agenda. While there is considerable dispute about exactly what is meant by action research, a central feature is that the research does not end with interpretation or theoretical understanding but makes the further step into action for the improvement of a situation, followed by the monitoring of the results of this action (see Robson, 1993, pp. 438-42).

Practitioner-centred action research puts practitioners in charge of all aspects of the evaluation. The role of a researcher or evaluator is as a consultant, and not as a controlling superior. As King puts (1995, p. 89) it 'in practitioner-centred action research, it is more important to answer the right questions, however messy the methodology, than to answer the wrong question extremely well. Issues of utility and feasibility sometimes demand trade-offs in technical accuracy.' This quotation helps give the flavour of the model, but it could be argued the same criteria should apply to all types of evaluation. It shares essentially the same advantages and disadvantages as participatory evaluation, possibly to a more extreme extent. In both cases the long-term aim can be seen as the 'withering away' of the specialist evaluator when the local personnel have achieved sufficient confidence and expertise to do it for themselves.

This end-state has similarities to the 'teacher research' model advocated by Laurence Stenhouse, and subsequently developed by John Elliott (1991) at the University of East Anglia in the UK. Teachers as practitioners are held to have the necessary skills and experience to carry out a worthwhile evaluation of their practice, typically without the need for someone with a technical evaluative background. The extent to which this claim has been justified is a matter of considerable debate (see Atkinson and Delamont, 1985).

Critical Evaluation

An additional participatory model with action research leanings is based on critical theory. Here the objective is to bring staff or other participants to an 'emancipatory' understanding of the context in which they work so they are in a position to debate the value of policies, practices and programs. This model is in part a reaction to concerns that evaluation is becoming more of a mechanism for managerial control rather than for change in the direction of greater equality and justice. It draws upon critical social science and postmodernist understandings of knowledge, truth and power.

This is a conflict model. Practitioners, either with the assistance of the evaluator or working autonomously, seek to analyse organizational practices with a view to transforming them. The role of management and administrative staff in this process is problematic, particularly if they are directly involved in the evaluation. It may lead to what Huberman (1995, p. 105) describes as ' a surreal situation, with the hierarchical chiefs firing up their subordinates in directions they would have preferred them to ride away from'.

Everitt and Hardiker (1996) develop this model in the context of social work and provide a range of case studies based upon their own research.

Using Consultants

Even if you are an experienced evaluator, it may well be helpful to get consultant advice of a variety of kinds. If you are new to the evaluation game then probably the most useful consultant is an experienced evaluator. This is a serious point. Reading a book like this can help you to appreciate many of the issues involved in designing and carrying out an evaluation but inevitably you have to make the difficult transition to your own specific situation and talking over your tentative proposals with someone who has done it all before will not only boost your confidence, but also help you to avoid some of the pitfalls.

Other non-evaluator experts fall into two main groups. First those who can provide the kind of consultant advice which is likely to be needed in many evaluations. For example if you have quantitative data and are no statistical expert yourself, then it is no shame to call on the services of a statistician. Many organizations have such persons hiding somewhere and it is worth seeking them out. The main problem is in communicating your needs. Statisticians should be good at finding out what their clients really need. Some are but unfortunately quite a number are not. Similarly if you have a substantial amount of qualitative data and have not had experience of analysing this kind of data, then you can save yourself much time and heart-ache by getting help from someone who has. It is a field which has developed tremendously over the last decade or so and university departments of social science should be able to link you to the relevant expertise. (For evaluations in specific areas it may be more profitable to contact the related departments, e.g. education, management, health care, social work, etc.)

Virtually all evaluations call for the production of a printed report and/or some other means of communicating the findings. An excellent evaluation can be seriously let down by a poor report. Chapter 7 goes into some detail on how you can avoid this situation and communicate with the intended audience(s). However, if you have access to persons with these skills, then by all means make use of their expertise.

The second type of consultant is specific to the particular evaluation.

For example if you are evaluating a new reading program, then apart from the usual stakeholders such as administrators, teachers and other program staff, parents and students, it could be helpful to call on consultants in fields such as curriculum development, reading, psychometrics, etc. The consultants' advice is probably most useful at the design stage (of both the program and its evaluation) in setting standards and developing evaluation questions. Obviously, the appropriateness and feasibility of drawing upon such consultants will depend very much upon your situation. Sufficient consultant knowledge may already exist within the team. Or you may not have finance available or be able to persuade a consultant to help you without payment.

Some kinds of evaluation make use of consultants in rather different ways. For example, the use of *expert panels* is something seen extensively in fields such as health or medicine. The intention is to assist in consensus development in areas where there are controversial topics and unresolved conflicts. This is an approach which appears most likely to be used at national or international level and not in small-scale evaluations. Fink (1995, pp. 39-43) discusses this topic and provides guidelines for the effective running of expert panels.

Persuading Practitioners to be Involved

Why should practitioners bother to be involved? Typically health-care workers, teachers and other professionals are very busy people, often under considerable stress. Taking part in an evaluation may be an additional task too far, especially if it carries the risk that any findings might be used to make life even more difficult. For those playing a direct role in the evaluation, there is likely to be aggravation and fatigue simply because they are doing different and additional tasks. Even when, as should always happen, a time allowance is made, practitioners can show stress and anxiety simply because they are spending some time away from their 'real' job.

Typically other stakeholders do not present the same difficulties. Policy and decision-makers can see a potentially useful outcome from the evaluation. Your problem is more likely to be in delivering an evaluation which is actually utilized by them. Sponsors may well have an emotional as well as a financial interest in the study. After all they chose you and it will not rebound well on them if the evaluation bombs. The clients could be more of a problem, but in many cases they will be very positive about an involvement particularly if it is seen as a scarce resource. The 'interested others', neighbours, persons involved in programs effectively competing for resources, and so on, will be only too glad to get their voice heard.

Figure 2.1 lists some of the potential benefits to practitioners from involvement in an evaluation. Whether such benefits outweigh the costs outlined above will obviously depend on the specifics of the situation. My experience suggests it is not so much the heaviness of the work-load,

- Professional development, particularly in relation to the skills of systematic inquiry. Many find that the data gathering and analysis involved are useful transferable skills for their other professional activities.
- Professional and personal empowerment. Evaluation and research are commonly regarded as high-status activities.
- Creation of leadership roles. The evaluation can provide an opportunity for practitioners to take on new and interesting roles (note however that the possible disappearance of such roles on conclusion of the project can cause problems).
- Development of new perspective. An evaluation perspective is added to one's professional tool-box, perhaps fostering the growth of a more 'reflective' professional (Schon, 1983; 1987).
- Sense of accomplishment. An evaluation is typically a finite and relatively short-term activity and its successful completion leads to a sense of achievement.
- Sharpening of critical eye. Participating in an evaluation can open the eyes of practitioners who have perhaps been coasting for a period after getting on top of the job without querying their current practice.
- Enjoyment. Yes, it can definitely be fun!
- Formation of personal and professional friendships. This can be part of the enjoyment. The coming together of stakeholders with different but linking interests, as well as working perhaps with a somewhat different group of colleagues, provides a good context for the making of friends – and without the kind of negative associations of the office party.
- Promotion to posts of additional responsibility. Involvement with an evaluation can provide a helpful test-bed for someone to earn their spurs. And it will help on the CV.
- Reawakening of interest in the job, and/or in evaluation and research. It is a new challenge where perhaps things have been humdrum. Also it is not unknown for practitioners to appreciate that they would like to transform themselves into evaluators or researchers, who will probably be all the better from their practitioner background.

Figure 2.1   *Potential benefits for practitioners from involvement in evaluations*

Source: Based in part on Cousins and Earl (1995, Chap. 10) which summarizes the findings of the set of participatory evaluations in Cousins and Earl (1995).

but factors like staff morale, quality of leadership and their experience of any previous evaluation or research which are more crucial. Researchers who are perceived as using the setting for their own research purposes without giving something back can effectively inoculate it against any further evaluation or research involvement. Figure 2.2 gathers together some suggestions about what might be done to avoid some likely problems when staff act as participants.

When is some Form of Participatory Evaluation Indicated?

The case for some kind of stakeholder involvement in an evaluation seems irrefutable, particularly one where there is a focus on utilization. However, deciding to take the further step where practitioners, and possibly other key stakeholders, become active participants in the evaluation

- Deliver on promises about what will happen and when it will happen (which calls for a realistic, feasible and adequately resourced evaluation plan). In a participant evaluation you inevitably hand over part of the responsibility to run the evaluation to others, but nevertheless your general efficiency and professionalism (assuming both of these are of high quality) will inevitably influence the running of the evaluation.
- Allow for adequate release time from normal duties to deal with time taken up by involvement with the evaluation. A GENERAL FINDING IS THAT THIS TIME REQUIREMENT TENDS TO BE UNDER-ESTIMATED.
- Recognise the possibility that participants will be viewed by colleagues as a privileged élite and seek to avoid this (e.g. by ensuring there are general benefits to the organisation from involvement with the evaluation).
- Avoid the really problematic settings (e.g. where the organization is under severe strain, or morale is very poor) – unless, of course, the focus of the evaluation is on really problematic settings!
- Work hard on utilization – frustration will occur if there is no action taken on the findings of an evaluation. Stressing this likely frustration to policy and decision-makers should in itself facilitate their utilization of the findings.

Figure 2.2   *Avoiding problems when staff act as participants in the evaluation*

should be the basis for serious consideration. While there do seem to be strong potential spin-offs, it is not without substantial costs. The organization will have to devote staff and other resources to activities over and above their normal tasks, while these continue unabated. Under what conditions does this appear to be both feasible and sensible? The following analysis relies heavily on Cousins and Earl (1995, pp. 174-8).

Top-down versus bottom-up approaches. There is strong evidence that the most successful approaches to change in organizations use a balance of top-down and bottom-up (Earl and Cousins, 1995). Top-down, where initiatives come from the top level of organizations, are based on broad policy perspectives of the future, hopefully but by no means necessarily, informed by theoretical considerations or empirical evidence. Bottom-up approaches, coming as it were from the shop-floor, are sensitive to local considerations but can suffer from focusing on limited, conservative changes and a failure to question basic assumptions.

Selection of participants. A central principle is that participants should be those who want to participate. Substantial preparatory work may be required, in particular so that the benefits of involvement can be appreciated. However, taking an active part in an evaluation is no sinecure and 'volunteering' people against their wishes is a recipe for trouble. As with most things ready volunteers provide a necessary but not sufficient criterion for choice. You are looking for those with the motivation to complete the task, and a good track-record for completion. The task will call for teamwork and there should be a balance of participants from different levels and areas of the organization. It is crucial to include those who are in an organizational position to implement any proposed changes arising from the evaluation, both because it is a direct part of their every-day work and because they are in a position to recommend and/or require such changes.

You would do well also to get on board any interested persons with expertise relevant to the evaluation. While your task as evaluator includes helping those without an evaluation or research background to make a worthwhile contribution, it helps all round if someone with, say, experience in interviewing or in data analysis is present.

Pre-existing partnerships. It is something of a truism to observe that a successful participatory evaluation is likely where you and the organization concerned have a previous history of working together well. Thus, the in-house evaluator held in high esteem in his organization starts something new with much both in his favour, and in favour of a successful evaluation. The general point is there is both short-term and long-term advantage in the development of strong connections and relationships between evaluators and those in practice. This calls for something of a re-evaluation of the approach taken by evaluators, and an internalization of 'evidence-based' practices within organizations.

Realistic appreciation of the costs involved. A consistent finding in the studies reported in Cousins and Earl (1995) is the underestimation of the time involved by participants in the evaluations. This is such a general finding, also showing up in many other areas of applied research, that one is tempted to suggest an universal doubling of time estimates. However, a thorough detailed working through of the implications of the evaluation plan, together with avoiding the temptation to give an estimate on the low side in order not to frighten sponsors, can produce more realistic estimates. Avoiding an underestimate is central to maintaining good relations throughout the life of the project.

Carrying out a pre-evaluation assessment. It is worth while to carry out a pre-evaluation assessment of an organization's readiness for working in this participatory way. Positive indicators include:

- Evidence for decision processes which truly value input from those responsible for the implementation of innovation.
- Practitioners already invited to assume leadership roles in the organization.
- A high degree of autonomy in decision-making at that level of the organization which is the focus of the evaluation.
- Openness to input from practitioners in combination with administration.

Chapter 2: Tasks

1. Who are the stakeholders in your evaluation? (May include *policy/ decision-makers; sponsors; management: staff/practitioners; clients/ service users; and interested others.*) Most of these will be pretty obvious, but the 'interested others' may need some thought.

2. What steps will you take to make sure all these stakeholders will have a voice? If you propose not to involve some of them, say why.
3. Do you propose to go beyond stakeholder involvement to a more participatory style of evaluation for your study?

    *   If *yes*, explain which (participatory/practitioner-centred action research/critical evaluation).
    *   If *no*, explain why you do not consider it suitable or feasible.

4. List the potential benefits to practitioners of being involved in this evaluation.

5. What are likely problems participants will face as a result of their involvement? How do you propose to deal with them (the participants as well as the problems!)?

3
ETHICAL AND POLITICAL
CONSIDERATIONS

Evaluation is inextricably linked to ethical and political issues. As has already been stressed, an important consideration when agreeing to carry out an evaluation is the existence of an intention to use the findings in some way. Typically the intended use is by makers of policy when making decisions about the program being evaluated. There is, of course, no guarantee the findings will actually be used. Policy-making is by definition political. A small-scale evaluation focusing on some possible change of practice in a work setting concerns the exercise of power which can affect the working life and conditions of those involved. Evaluations in public services are linked to social policies and priorities, at root deriving from party political (Politics with a large P) initiatives, as well as within-service uses of power.

Cheetham et al. (1992, p. 149) discuss these links in the context of social work where there is an attempt to do something about societal problems such as poverty, ill-health, disability and relationships in peril. As they say:

> Since the responses to such troubles are often both contentious and ill-resourced, social work, by its association with them, can reap the whirlwind. Thus, when care management falls apart and old people deteriorate in residential care or their daughters collapse from overwork or anxiety, when children are killed by their parents or removed from them, amid cries of protest, when supportive services fail to prevent deterioration or disaster, so will the storms break around the world of social work.

Any evaluation of these services is obviously and inherently tangling with extremely sensitive ethical and political issues. It is interesting to note that the statement of principles in the British Association of Social Workers' code of ethics which outlines social workers' professional obligation to 'increase personal knowledge and skill . . . and to contribute to the total body of professional knowledge' adds to this the requirement for 'constant evaluation of methods and policies in the light of changing needs' (nd, para. 8). Or as Cheetham et al. (1992, p. 5) put it 'social workers know that they must ask and answer the question "what is the use of what I'm doing?" ' Increasingly, this requirement to evaluate practice is being viewed as an ethical necessity in professions dealing with people.

Ethical Issues

Evaluations deal with issues which affect people's lives. It is a minimum requirement they should be carried out to a high standard. Various attempts have been made to specify just what this might mean. For example there are *Program Evaluation Standards* published by the Joint Committee on Standards (1994). This, as with most such efforts, is American and is reprinted as Appendix C. It covers four areas, summarized in Figure 3.1. Other attempts to codify standards have been made by the Evaluation Research Society (1982) and the American Evaluation Association (1995). These are also provided as appendices in Newman and Brown (1996).

As discussed in Chapter 2, there are different stakeholders each with an interest in an evaluation. These interests must be recognized and respected if the evaluation is to be carried out in an ethically responsible manner. Fortunately, taking serious note of this in planning and running the study carries the bonus that it is both more likely to be of high quality with well focused evaluation questions, and to be made use of subsequently. Apart from this very general concern for different interests, there are more specific safeguards to be addressed for the clients or users of the program or service, as well as staff and other participants directly involved with its running. Three main aspects need to be considered – *consent, privacy and confidentiality,* and *risks as related to benefits.*

Utility. Evaluations should be useful in the sense that they serve the information needs of intended users and are carried out in such a way that the likelihood the evaluation will be used is increased.

Feasibility. Evaluations should be realistic, prudent, diplomatic and frugal.

Propriety. Evaluations should be conducted legally, ethically and with due regard for the welfare of those involved in the evaluation, as well as those affected by its results.

Accuracy. Evaluations should reveal and convey technically adequate information about features that determine the worth or merit of the program being evaluated.

Figure 3.1   *Program evaluation standards.*

Source: From Joint Committee on Standards (1994).

Consent

It is a general ethical principle that you do not seek to evaluate, or have take part in an evaluation, anyone who either does not know they are involved or does not wish to take part. This is usually referred to as the principle of *voluntary informed consent.* There is much to be said for using a formal consent form although this does depend on circumstances. I have the suspicion that sometimes the form is used more for the protection of evaluators and their organizations (not a negligible consideration of course) than to safeguard the interests of clients or participants. Generally, it isn't appropriate to seek formal consent when it is straightforward for people to refuse (for example with a postal questionnaire where the rubbish bin provides an easy solution). Similarly there are situations perhaps involving illegal or dubious activities where it is highly unlikely written consent would be given, and it would be unwise of the evaluator to keep a record of individual identities.

Title or name of evaluation:

Taking part in this study is on a voluntary basis. You can withdraw from it at any time if you wish. You don't need to give a reason and there will be no penalty. Nevertheless we do hope you will continue to be involved and find the experience worth while.

The only commitment on your part is to be interviewed about your views on how the project is going and the effects it has had on yourself and colleagues. The interview will last between half an hour and forty minutes and will be taped so we can get an accurate record of your views. This will be completely confidential. A written transcript of the interview will be made and you are welcome to see this and correct any misunderstandings, or add further comments.

This account will only be seen by myself and, possibly, two colleagues. In any report or other feedback to the company, it will be ensured that all views and comments from the interviews are anonymous, so it will not be possible for individuals to be recognized.

Thank you for agreeing to take part.

Name and title:

Address and phone number:

I have read the information provided and agree to be interviewed:

_____   _____

Signature   Date

Please print name here

Figure 3.2 *Example of a consent form*

Figure 3.2 gives an example, indicating the kinds of things included in a consent form. The following aspects are important:

- The language should be simple and friendly, taking note of the audience. It is as important not to be patronizing as it is to be understandable.

- In translating the central idea of the evaluation into understandable language, the key is to omit jargon and details not important to the reader, whilst including details they do need to know relating directly to their own involvement (particularly exactly what that will be, and how long it will take).

The form itself is only a part of a process. Simply because they have signed a form doesn't mean they fully understand what they have let themselves in for. As the evaluation continues, they may develop misgivings. Or their circumstances may change and they find the demands too onerous.

Because they present as volunteers doesn't guarantee their true voluntary status. This is most likely to be an issue in situations where you can predict there will be implicit, or even explicit, pressure to be involved. This is particularly so with 'captive' groups (not necessarily just those in prison), employees and others who anticipate possible favours from their participation or penalties from their refusal. Sieber (1992; 1998), who has presented very detailed and helpful suggestions for carrying out ethically responsible research, points out: 'An individual's understanding of the consent statement and acceptance of his or her status as an autonomous decision maker will be most powerfully influenced not by what the individual is told, but by how he or she is engaged in the communication.' (1998, p. 131).

Your general attitude will make a considerable difference. Friendliness, respect and empathy will convey as much, probably more, than the actual words you use. If those you are working with feel you are worthy of trust, they will be prepared to open up to you and reveal their true views and feelings. Obtaining such trust can be particularly difficult if you are perceived to be of higher status or are from a different social, ethnic or age group. If feasible, there is much to be said for an interviewer or observer sharing important characteristics of these kinds with those being interviewed or observed.

It may help if you provide them with a sheet giving some details of yourself and your background and how you can be contacted, perhaps with a photograph if you are going to be around and not everyone will know who you are.

Debriefing. In research involving people it is good practice to follow up a session where information has been gathered from them with a further session where there is discussion about the research and how an individual's contribution fits into this. It provides an opportunity for research subjects to give general views and perceptions of the experience they have just been through. In settings such as schools and hospitals, staff often appreciate the chance to talk about their practice with someone who is obviously interested and, sometimes erroneously, considered to be an expert. From the point of view of the researcher this can be very revealing, providing suggestions for improvement of the study.

This kind of debriefing may also be appropriate, for the same kind of reasons, in some evaluations. One situation where it is essential is when any form of deception has been practised on the people involved. In experimental work, attempts are sometimes made to justify deception on the grounds that if the subject knew the real focus of the research, this would distort or make impossible the collection of data. Examples such as Milgram's (1963) notorious studies of obedience where people thought they were administering increasingly severe electric shocks to others illustrate both deception and why this is ethically dubious.

Deceit has little or no part to play in evaluation and certainly should not be used to trick people into being involved when if they did know what was really involved they would have been unlikely to take part. A possible exception could be in some designs where there are different conditions, e.g. in studies where there is a control or 'placebo' condition, in addition to some form of 'treatment' condition whose effectiveness is the focus of the evaluation. Telling them from the start to which condition they have been assigned negates the whole purpose of the design. Here a solution is to inform all concerned there are these different conditions and they will be thoroughly debriefed at the end of the study.

Privacy

Privacy is concerned with respect for an individual's wish to have control over access to themselves and information about themselves. While we are likely to have a clear idea about what we would wish to keep private, and what would be a violation of that privacy, it is more difficult to judge this in relation to others. This is particularly so when they are different from you, say in gender, sexual orientation or ethnic background. It is clearly ethically questionable to intrude. Intrusion will also make it likely that people will not co-operate, or will be defensive or evasive – all of which is likely to affect the quality of the evaluation.

The voluntary nature of their involvement acknowledges a right to privacy which can be exercised by refusing to take part in the study. Also, if the principle of voluntary informed consent is honoured, the related issues of confidentiality and anonymity can and should be covered.

Confidentiality. This concerns information about a person (such as interview transcripts, notes, or video- or audiotapes) and an agreement about how this information will be treated to respect their privacy.

Anonymity. This refers to ensuring that a person's name, or other unique identifier, is not attached to information about that person.

If an informed consent form is used, it should make it clear how each of these aspects will be dealt with. If one is not used then similar reassurances should be made verbally and, of course, honoured. Figure 3.3 covers a number of points relevant to privacy and confidentiality. Some of these might not be relevant in a particular evaluation but it is worth

- How will the people's names be obtained, and will they be told about where you got them from?
- Will they be able to opt in to the evaluation (such as by returning a card if they wish to volunteer)?
- Opt out methods (such as asking people to 'phone to cancel a visit) can be intrusive.
- Is it reasonable to send reminders, or can this seem coercive?
- Will sessions directly with individuals be conducted in a quiet, private place?
- Can a friend be present or absent as the respondent prefers?
- In rare cases, if evaluators think they must report confidential replies, such as when they think someone is in danger, will they try to discuss this first with the respondent?
- Do they warn all respondents this might happen?
- Will personal names be changed in records and in reports to hide the subjects' identity?
- What should evaluators do if subjects prefer to be named in reports?
- Will the evaluation records, notes, tapes, films or videos be kept in lockable storage space?
- Who will have access to these records, and be able to identify the subjects? (Using post codes only does not protect anonymity.)
- When significant extracts from interviews are quoted in reports, should evaluators first check the quotation and commentary with the person concerned?
- What should researchers do if respondents want the reports to be altered?
- Before evaluators spend time alone with children, should their police records be checked?
- Should evaluation records be destroyed when a project is completed, as market researchers are required to do?
- Is it acceptable to recontact the same respondents and ask them to take part in another project?

Figure 3.3 *Privacy and confidentiality issues*

Source: Adapted from Alderson (1996, pp. 107–8).

checking through the list to help think through exactly how you will treat the relevant issues.

It should not be automatically assumed that confidentiality and anonymity have to be part of an evaluation. What is crucial is that any undertakings made should be honoured scrupulously. It may not be feasible to give such undertakings in some situations. A small-scale evaluation in a particular setting could have such a limited cast of actors that their roles and likely views are widely known – at least in that setting. It is possible to alter unimportant details (although what counts as unimportant is open to question) and hence blur the picture, but this is only worth while if lack of anonymity worries the people involved.

Confidentiality and anonymity can be seen in negative terms. It may be depriving workers and others of legitimate kudos or publicity for delivering an exceptionally effective or innovative service. Even what might be seen as calling for anonymity by most people may not appear in that way to a particular person. Sieber (1998, p. 138) cites a case study of a well-known 'fence' described by Klockars (1974). This individual who had dealt with very large amounts of stolen goods in a long career in crime would only agree to participate in the study if his real name and address were used and the entire account published.

Restrictions on Confidentiality

There are legal limits to promises of confidentiality. Obvious examples are in the fields of child abuse and neglect, and of threats of harm to oneself or others. It is, of course, important you know the legal situation in which you are working, and that you have thought through your stance towards it. While some might argue for a blanket statement that disclosure of any law-breaking activity would not be considered as covered by confidentiality, such a stance would rule out a number of fields of study such as soft drug use by young people.

Any consent form should make it very clear if there are types of information which, if made available to you, would lead to your approaching the police or other relevant authority. Generally, evaluators and other researchers do not have the kind of protection available to the legal and medical professions and to ministers of religion, who can refuse to reveal their sources of information.

Confidentiality and Accountability

One solution to problems of ensuring confidentiality is to destroy data such as tapes and interview transcripts immediately after they have been used for analysis and interpretation. However, there is increasingly an expectation from the point of view of research ethics that such data should be available for inspection. Only if this is done can there be a direct check on the veracity of data reported and the reasonableness of the interpretation made.

This is, perhaps, less of an issue with small-scale evaluations where reporting is typically to a local non-specialist audience. However, as discussed in Chapter 7, this should not preclude some other, additional, form of publication such as in a professional journal. Here an editor could well ask to see raw data. If this more formal type of publication is a possibility, then it is best to avoid promises of early data destruction. Given current concerns about data fabrication, this is a helpful move towards allowing greater data checking.

Anonymity does not create problems for this kind of data checking and every effort should be made to remove any identifiers which could lead to the recognition of individuals.

Linking Data

Collecting and maintaining data which have been anonymized make it difficult to link together different data sets so that contributions from particular individuals can be recognized and put together. This kind of matching can be done by constructing codes unique to each person. For example, the last two letters from their first name and the day and month of their birthday (e.g. IN2707) could be used. Any scheme of this type is open to abuse by the evaluator or data analyst. There is no substitute for integrity on your part, and the trust of participants has to be earned through your general approach and track record.

An alternative is to employ a 'broker' who is responsible for linking the various sets of data. Such a person has to be trusted by participants and yourself to do the job both without disclosing identities to you, and without making mistakes (because you are not going to be able to check!).

Risk in Relation to Benefit

Risk. Anything anybody does carries with it some element of risk. For most small-scale evaluations, the risk of physical harm is minimal. It is probably comparable to that encountered in general in people's every-day private and working lives. What is more likely is some kind of social, psychological or even financial risk. For example taking part in an evaluation may perhaps sensitize individuals to negative aspects of their work situation, leading to depression and upset. The evaluation, or the way in which its findings are used, may lead to changes in the work situation, even at the extreme to the closure of a service and the loss of a job.

There is an onus on the evaluator not to get involved in various kinds of pseudo-evaluation, for example where it is being used simply to facilitate the making of administrative decisions such as closing down a service or centre. However, even legitimate evaluations may carry with them the possibility of negative consequences for some of those involved. Obviously, if there are possibilities of serious harm or damage, whether physical, psychological, social or legal, these should be thought through and the situation made clear to any potential participants.

Assessing risk is not a straightforward or simple task. It is helpful to discuss possible risks with the various stakeholders to get different perspectives, particularly if you are working in a field where you don't have extensive prior experience. Attention should be given to those who are likely to be vulnerable and most at risk. These include:

- Anyone without power, or with diminished power, in the situation (e.g. persons in institutions such as prisons and hospitals).
- Those who might be damaged by the process of the evaluation, or by implementation of the findings.
- People in the public eye, or who might be placed in the public eye as a result of the evaluation.
- Children and others who can't speak for themselves.
- Law-breakers and those who might be harmed if their activities were made public.

One risk sometimes met by evaluations is for the findings or recommendations to be misused or misrepresented. Newspapers or other media may give simplistic accounts or misleading headlines. A sensible pre-emptive strategy here is to prepare a press release in appropriate language (i.e. language which a busy reporter can lift directly and use as copy). Worse in some ways is the risk that policy or decision-makers might, deliberately or not, place a perverse interpretation on the findings. There is no total safeguard against this, but building up good relations with them during the evaluation and working for their active involvement make it less likely.

Benefit. We are concerned here with the possible benefits of the evaluation, rather than benefits of the program which is being evaluated. In considering potential benefits to weigh against the risks of the evaluation, it is helpful to pit likely benefits for particular stakeholders against the risks they run. Table 3.1 gives a benefit table covering both those with a close involvement and wider audiences.

The broader horizons of potential benefits to society and science are not to be totally ignored, but more immediate benefits to key stakeholders particularly practitioners and other participants should be the main focus. This recognizes that even if they have not been at any real risk by being involved, they are likely to have been inconvenienced and, possibly, stressed. It has the pragmatic advantage that, if such benefits are experienced, the chances of a positive outcome to the evaluation will be improved. The setting will also be more receptive to future initiatives.

Table 3.1 categorizes seven types of benefit, ranging from those which are relatively easy to provide, to ones which would be quite unusual in a small-scale evaluation. For example, looked at in the context of the institution or service which has been the focus of the evaluation, potential benefits might be:

- *Relationships*: links are established or developed with helping institutions such as university departments or in-house evaluation and research services.
- *Knowledge*: there is improved understanding of the problems and issues they face.
- *Material resources*: possible provision of materials, equipment and funding linked to the evaluation.
- *Training*: staff and other practitioners enhance their skills, particularly if it is a participative type of evaluation.
- *Doing good*: through taking part in the evaluation the institution learns how to serve its clients better.
- *Empowerment*: findings from the evaluation can be used both for policy and publicity purposes, leading to favourable attention from the media, central administrators and politicians.
- *Scientific outcomes*: given a successful evaluation, there is increased confidence in the validity of the program or service.

Even if the evaluation casts doubt on the effectiveness of a new program,

Table 3.1 *Benefit table for an evaluation*

Benefit	Practitioners and other participants	Organization/community	Sponsor	Evaluator
Relationships	Respect of evaluator and other stakeholders	Ties to evaluator and her organization	Ties with a successful project	Future access to organization/community
Knowledge/education	Informative debriefing	Understanding of relevant learning problems	Outstanding final report	Knowledge
Material resources	Various, e.g. access to program materials, work books, etc.	Books	Instructional material	Grant support
Training opportunity	Tutoring skills	Trained practitioners	Model project for future grant applications	Greater evaluative expertise
Do good/earn esteem	Esteem of peers	Local enthusiasm for project	Satisfaction of funder overseers	Respect from colleagues
Empowerment	Earn leadership status	Prestige from the project	Increase in funding	Enhanced reputation with funder
Scientific/clinical success	Improved learning ability	Effective program	Proven success of funded treatment	Publications

Source: Slightly adapted from Sieber (1998, p. 150).

many of the other benefits still accrue. It is helpful to think in benefit terms from the early stages as it may well be possible to 'tweak' the design to optimize the benefits to those involved. It is quite legitimate to ensure they appreciate both the immediate benefits from involvement as well as likely longer-term ones.

Assessing benefits relative to risk in an evaluation is not an exact science. One might be dubious about proceeding if any benefits were heavily skewed towards particular stakeholders (say if management looked likely to show major benefits and there seemed to be nothing in it for the workforce). However, the main requirement is that everyone has a realistic appreciation of both likely risks and likely benefits when they give their informed consent.

The Problem of Unintended Consequences

The history of social interventions includes a worryingly large number of instances of cases where programs introduced with totally benign intentions turned out to have seriously negative consequences for those involved. McCord (1978), evaluating a preventative program focusing on delinquent youths, found the treatments actually produced psychological and behavioural effects which were self-defeating for those involved. A program which was successful in preventing the negative consequences of divorce could well make it easier for people to consider divorce. Or programs concentrating on reducing the negative consequences of addiction to drugs or alcohol might lead to an increase in drug or alcohol abuse.

Evaluation itself can provide a means of exposing such unintended effects, and possibly of suggesting ways in which they might be reduced. However, the evaluation itself can well have unintended consequences. For example it may lead to anticipatory stress on the part of those involved. This can take extreme forms such as loss of sleep or eating disorders. Clearly this is not intended by the evaluator and it is likely that by establishing good relationships with participants, advance warning of such sensitivities can be gained and measures taken to reduce them. Other effects are more difficult to predict in advance and hence are not readily included in any listing of the potential risks run by participants.

Some consequences of evaluation, while not directly intended, can be beneficial. The knowledge that a program or service is the subject of an evaluation can in itself lead to an improvement in the way in which it is delivered. This is a version of the so-called Hawthorne effect (Parsons, 1974; Bramel and Friend, 1981). It constitutes a benefit as far as the recipients of the program are concerned, but it is a problem when seeking to provide an unbiased picture of the effectiveness of the program. Logically it is not possible to evaluate this without an evaluation!

One view, not without attraction, is that if the fact that something is being evaluated in itself leads to its improvement, then why not incorporate evaluation routinely? The counter-arguments are that such routinized procedures will to a large extent habituate those involved, and that a routine full-blown evaluation would not be feasible in resource terms. A possibility is to develop systems where some minimal set of evaluative procedures is routinely followed.

Evaluations Involving Children and other Vulnerable Populations

Ethical issues are brought into sharp focus when children are involved. Most legal systems seek to ensure they have special protection, and also that the rights of their parents or guardians are respected. There are several reasons for this, including:

- They are, by definition, immature emotionally, intellectually and socially.
- People such as teachers, health and social workers, parents and evaluators have substantial power over them.
- They may not be able to give meaningful informed consent, perhaps because of an inability to understand what is involved.

Obviously it is essential you work within both the letter and the spirit of the law. However, it is also necessary for any evaluation involving children to be informed by knowledge about child development so that potential risk can be understood and reduced. This may call for the services of a specialized consultant.

The difficulties children, particularly younger ones, have in giving informed consent should not be used as an excuse for not seeking such consent. The language used and the details of the procedure (such as their assent being asked for by someone they know and trust) should be carefully tailored to their social and cognitive level of development.

The general principle is that both the child and the parent or guardian should give their consent. If either does not agree, then you do not proceed. There may be some situations where it is ethical to proceed without parental permission, for example when the parent or guardian is not acting in the child's best interests (see Sieber, 1992, pp. 112–14). However, this gets one into very difficult areas bearing in mind you are an interested party and it is wisest to stick to the dual approval rule.

There are other vulnerable groups such as the mentally handicapped or disturbed, drug abusers, victims of violence, etc. Programs and services frequently seek to target such groups as they tend to be regarded as social problems where 'something must be done'. The points made above about consent, privacy and the weighing up of risk and benefit apply with particular force when evaluating programs for these groups. An added complication is that some groups may be unfavourably disposed towards evaluation and evaluators. It is unlikely to go down well with them if you strike an objective, detached, 'scientific' stance. From a pragmatic standpoint you are more likely to obtain co-operation and trust by making it clear you are committed to help find ways of improving their lot. There is a difficult balance to achieve here, which will differ from one situation to another. It is counterproductive to be openly partisan which may lead to conclusions and proposals for action not firmly based in the available evidence. It may also alienate policy-makers and administrators who mistrust your judgement. Renzetti and Lee (1993) give valuable advice on working in such sensitive situations.

Ethical Boards and Committees

It is increasingly common for there to be a requirement for an evaluation plan to be formally approved by an ethical board or committee. In the USA, universities and similar institutions have institutional review boards (IRBs) and there is federal and state law setting formal hurdles. Similar institutional arrangements are now in place in many universities in the UK, and corresponding committees have existed in medical and health-care settings for many years.

Typically a detailed plan for the evaluation has to be submitted, with particular focus on the ethical issues and how they are to be dealt with. There is likely to be a protocol or checklist which should obviously be followed closely. Sieber (1992) provides an extensive list which covers several features specific to the North American context. Alderson (1996, pp. 106-12) gives a similar list of topics for an ethics review from a UK perspective. Points specific to privacy and confidentiality are as listed in Figure 3.3.

There can be difficulties when the list is modelled on the design of experiments and other highly structured approaches, and a more open and flexible design seems appropriate to answer the evaluation questions. The politics of this situation dictate you must satisfy the requirements of an ethical board, but it is a great pity if this acts as a Procrustean bed forcing inappropriate design changes. One strategy is to make it clear what is presented is a scenario, giving the best current guess about detailed matters such as how many participants and clients will be taking part, the number and nature of interview and observation sessions, etc.

This should be acceptable, providing the necessarily tentative nature of what is proposed is made clear. There may be a condition imposed on any approval that a definitive proposal is submitted at some later date. This is preferable to modifying the design in an inappropriate manner, or of taking the unethical step of changing the design to fit in with prejudices of a committee, and then going ahead with what you originally proposed!

Ethical Aspects of Evaluation Agreements

As discussed in the previous chapter, there is much to be said for having a written statement signed by the sponsor and yourself as evaluator. This lays down the general conditions under which the evaluation will take place and the expectations of both parties. It may overlap with the documentation which has to be prepared for an ethical board or committee, and in any case your agreement with the sponsor should be consistent with what you are saying to the ethical board.

Any agreement should cover the ethical issues discussed in this chapter. It can be valuable in helping you withstand later pressure to 'reveal your sources'. Naturally, once an agreement has been negotiated and signed, you and the other parties involved should stick to it.

The Politics of Evaluation

An evaluation is inevitably linked to policy and to political decisions. Should a program or service be stopped or continued? Should its budget and personnel be increased or cut back? There is a fundamental difference between the concerns of evaluators who evaluate other people's programs, and administrators and other personnel whose careers depend on them implementing and running successful programs. Campbell (1969) has suggested the resulting conflicts might be avoided if administrators took a scientific view focusing on the actual effectiveness of their programs and services, and evaluators restricted their evaluations to programs and not to people. Unfortunately, while clearly desirable this is something of a counsel of perfection. Administrators and politicians are not noted for taking an objective, scientific view even though researchers have long urged them to do so. Evaluators can endeavour to make it clear that their interest is in evaluating the program rather than the people involved, but the very fact that an evaluation is taking place increases the sensitivity of all involved who almost inevitably take it in personal terms. These political realities inevitably lead to difficulties in conducting objective evaluations, as detailed in Figure 3.4.

The partial answer is, as before, for the evaluator to take seriously the idea that stakeholders should have a role in the planning and, where pos-

1) Many evaluations carry the expectation that the evaluator will give advice and suggestions about improvement (even when this is not the main purpose of the evaluation). Most call for some type of report at the end. It is difficult for an evaluator to give an unbiased summary when the suggestions for improvement have been taken on board – and also when they haven't!
2) It is an important part of an evaluator's task to establish good relations with the various stakeholders involved. Personal relationships, rapport and empathy all help in building up the trust needed to obtain good-quality data. Unfortunately these processes also make it very difficult to be fully objective.
3) Negative results are likely to be unwelcome to the sponsors in many cases. They may show that money and resources have been wasted. Next time the sponsors might look for a more sympathetic evaluator.
4) Similarly if you have been employed by local administrators or staff there may be even greater pressure to report favourable outcomes.

Figure 3.4 *Political realities creating difficulties for objective evaluations*

sible, the running of evaluations. It can then be shaped to address their concerns, and they may well appreciate the benefits likely to arise from the evaluation.

Evaluators need to learn humility. As Mary James (1993, p. 135) puts it:

> The power of research-based evaluation to provide evidence on which rational decisions can be expected to be made is quite limited. Policy-makers will always find reasons to ignore, or be highly selective of, evaluation findings if the information does not support the particular political agenda operating at the time when decisions have to be made.

She is writing in the context of PRAISE (Pilot Records of Achievement in Schools Evaluation) which was a large-scale national project directly commissioned by the Department of Education and Science and the Welsh Office in the UK and funded to the tune of several million pounds sterling. However, in between the time the study was commissioned and the time of its completion, the political agenda and policy changed substantially (even though the same government was in control) and, effectively, the study was ignored. As she says 'political considerations will always provide convenient answers to awkward questions thrown up by research' (James, 1993, p. 119). Understandably disturbed by this clear demonstration of the illusory nature of an ideal of rational decision-making based on information derived from research-based evaluation, her suggestion is that the best evaluators can do when they discover their findings do not fit in with the current political agenda is to make public their evidence.

As illustrated by this example, the different timescales of evaluators and policy-makers provide a major reason for the non-use of evaluation findings. A relatively large-scale evaluation will probably extend over two or more years; policy-makers notoriously want answers yesterday. Even in the context of small-scale evaluations, with a timescale of a few months, this is still a real problem. Sanday (1993, p. 36) gives examples of evaluations carried out in local education authority schools, and makes the related point that 'the time-scale for research is long compared to that for policy-making and action with the result that developments are often disseminated before they have been adequately evaluated'.

The fact that many small-scale evaluations arise because of the personal advocacy of a policy-maker, whether administrator or local politician, can cause problems when the findings of the study are not to their liking. As Sanday points out, one of the few circumstances in which acceptance of a critical evaluation becomes possible is when its reception happens to coincide with a change of staff, or of political control.

The issue of how far an evaluator should get involved with the politics of the settings in which they work is not easy to resolve. An understanding of the social ecology of the organizations (how they 'work', who are the important 'players' and who the ones without influence, etc.) is central to many evaluations. However, putting a gloss on presentations or otherwise modifying your approach to an evaluation to take note of the micropolitics in, say, a local education or health authority prejudices your integrity as an evaluator and would be considered by some to be unethical.

Partisan evaluation. Taken to an extreme it becomes what Mohr (1995, p. 286) refers to as a partisan evaluation. In other words one carried out for particular sponsors and designed to serve their interests. The evaluation questions to be considered here are those whose inclusion is likely to be of benefit to the sponsors. This might include not only direct information adding to the weight of evidence in favour of a particular program or plan of action, but also to protect against counter-proposals. For example those wishing to evaluate a voucher system for public education with a view to its adoption could well benefit from evidence on opponents' claims that

> Vouchers could foster segregation by race and class, undermine the Constitutional separation of church and state, encourage hucksterism in the schools, increase the tax burden for public support of schooling, undermine existing systems of professional tenure for teachers and administrators, and destroy the shared democratic values fostered by the traditional system of public schools.
>
> (Weiler, 1976, p. 281)

In this situation the evaluator is essentially an adviser to a specific person or group and decisions about what should be included in the evaluation and any subsequent report depend on their concerns. This does not imply a licence to be unethical in the sense of being less rigorous in the planning and carrying out of the evaluation. In practice partisan evaluations are carried out very frequently. The position of the evaluator towards sponsor and public is very similar to that of the responsible accountant.

Public interest evaluation. An alternative stance is one where the evaluation aims to serve the public interest no matter who is paying for it, i.e. the evaluator is non-partisan. This implies a concern for the interests of all stakeholders, including in particular those with little power, and would be considered by many to be necessary if the evaluation is to be ethical in a wider sense.

Whichever stance is adopted, ignoring political realities may lead to policy-makers consigning the findings of an evaluation to oblivion. There are clear ethical problems about getting into an evaluation in which the aims include utilization, if you proceed in a way which seriously reduces the chances of any findings being used. As ever, the devil is in the detail of particular situations, but this is a genuine ethical dilemma.

In some ways, the knowledge that an evaluation is only one, possibly relatively minor, factor in a complex political process of balancing interests and reaching decisions is a comfort. And, of course, the evaluator is only one player in the evaluation itself, particularly when some participative styles of evaluation are used. As Rossi and Freeman (1993, p. 454) put it 'the evaluator's role is close to that of an expert witness, furnishing the best information possible under the circumstances; it is not the role of judge and jury'.

Chapter 3: Tasks

1. What are the main ethical issues raised by your proposed evaluation? For example obtaining consent, guaranteeing confidentiality and anonymity (if appropriate), risk (in relation to benefit)?

    Assume *all* evaluations will raise ethical issues. Discussions with stakeholders may help in bringing them to the surface. How do you propose to deal with these issues?

2. Produce a draft consent form or justify why you are not using one.

3. Find out what formal submissions have to be made to an ethical board or committee.

4. What potential problems arise from the political context for the conduct of the evaluation and subsequent implementation of findings? How can you minimise them?

Note:
If you find this difficult to consider in general terms, consider a possible specific finding of your evaluation and its political implications.

4

DESIGNS FOR DIFFERENT PURPOSES

Design refers to the overall strategy of the study. It is not the particular method or methods you will use, such as interviewing people, but more the general approach taken. As Catherine Hakim (1987, p. 1) puts it when talking about research design in general, stressing the similarities with building design:

> Design deals primarily with aims, uses, purposes, intentions and plans within the practical constraints of location, time, money and availability of staff. It is also very much about *style*, the architect's own preferences and ideas (whether innovative or solidly traditional) and the stylistic preferences of those who pay for the work and have to live with the final result.

The stress on practical constraints, and on the importance of taking serious note of the needs and wishes of others, apply with particular force when designing evaluations.

Evaluation Questions

The design depends crucially on the purpose of your evaluation. It will also differ depending on whether you are looking at a new program or one which is already well established. The decisions it seeks to inform also help to shape the design. Above all, it is shaped by the kind of questions to which you want answers. In one context the main question might be whether or not the program is being implemented in the way it was originally planned. Or it might be important to know whether it is reaching the desired client population. These are very different questions from ones concentrating on the effectiveness of the program in reaching stated goals or objectives. Different questions call for different designs.

How then does one get one's bearings in this mass of complexities? Figure 4.1 lists a number of common questions to which answers are sought. By coming to a provisional decision about which of them are most important for your evaluation you will begin to simplify the task. These are by no means the only questions which might be asked. Patton (1981) lists over a hundred types of evaluation linked to evaluation questions, which he distils down to 33 (1982, pp. 45–7). And there are other questions related more to the evaluation itself – such as 'what informa-

1) What is needed?
2) Does what is provided meet client needs?
3) What happens when it is in operation?
4) Does it attain its goals or objectives?
5) What are its outcomes?
6) How do costs and benefits compare?
7) Does it meet required standards?
8) Should it continue?
9) How can it be improved?

NB   The first question is relevant to a proposed program or service; the others
to ones already in operation.

Figure 4.1   *Some possible questions about a program, innovation,
intervention, project, service, etc.*

tion is needed by decision-makers when deciding about the future of the
program?'

Remember that when carrying out a small-scale evaluation you will
have to be strict about priorities. You might feel that, ideally, you would
wish to seek answers to many, or even all, of the questions, but it is highly
unlikely you will have the time and resources to do this.

What is needed? All too often program planners and service providers
have put on the new programs and services which they, in their wisdom,
thought were appropriate. They may then have been distressed to discover a poor response, either with few takers or with those who did
become involved showing dissatisfaction. The likelihood of this occurring can be reduced by means of a *needs analysis*. This involves gathering information about what are the currently unmet needs within a
community or organization through discussions with potential clients
and others likely to know what might be needed.

Does what is provided meet client needs? With new programs or services
it may be possible to build in a formal needs analysis as part of the initial
development work. This will make it more likely the needs of the clients
who form the target audience for the program or service are met, but in
no way guarantees it. Generally, the more 'top-down' the program or
service (i.e. the more it comes from on high, perhaps as a result of a government initiative) with less direct involvement of clients and potential
clients in its design, the more important to have this question on the
agenda. Unfortunately in such situations there may also be greater resistance to deploying resources to answer it. This will be particularly so if
it is suspected the answer may not be to the liking of sponsors of the
program or service.

The question of whether a program actually reaches the target audience is linked to this in that it is concerned with possible mismatches
between the audience and the program or service. For example a program
targeted at disadvantaged families may not be reaching them through the

literacy demands it makes, or its timing or accessibility. For some types of program, for example 'in-house' training for an organization, it should be possible to ensure the target audience is reached, at least in a physical sense.

What happens when it is in operation? Study of the processes involved when a program or service is in operation calls for a very different set of evaluation activities from a study focusing on outcomes or goal achievement, as discussed below. However, the two approaches can usefully complement each other. In particular, knowledge and understanding of day-to-day activities and processes may help to explain non-achievement of goals or unexpected outcomes. A specific concern which often repays attention is whether the intended program or service is actually implemented as planned.

Does it attain its goals or objectives? This is regarded by many as *the* evaluation question. Certainly it seems clear that if you set up some program with a particular declared purpose, then it would seem central to establish whether or not you have succeeded. It is also necessary to face up to the fact that many evaluations of social programs do not show positive results, or at best provide patchy and disappointing evidence that the program has attained its goals.

What are its outcomes? Are they, generally, favourable or do they reveal big differences between what was expected and achieved? Concentrating on the outcomes of a program or service is a broader question than whether goals or objectives are achieved, but they both share a 'black box' view. In other words the program or service is thought of as providing some kind of 'input' to the clients or participants. The task of the evaluation is to measure or otherwise assess the 'output'. However, given it may well be that the service leads to *unintended* outcomes, quite possibly unenvisaged ones, focusing on this question calls for a more open, exploratory, style of evaluation than one needed to assess the achievement of prespecified goals.

How do costs and benefits compare? This question can be asked either in an absolute sense or relative to some other program or service. When both costs and benefits are expressed in monetary terms this is known as *cost-benefit analysis*. When costs are expressed in monetary terms but benefits in non-monetary terms as *cost-effectiveness analysis*. This type of assessment of efficiency is likely to be of considerable interest to decision-makers but the question is seldom easy to answer.

Does it meet required standards? The formal accreditation or validation of programs or services is typically a matter of assuring that certain minimum requirements are met. There either tend to be detailed rules of procedure laid down to which evaluators must adhere, or it is assumed that commonsense notions are adequate and there is no need for any specialist evaluator expertise. This is a field which would benefit from such expertise, but the amount of time and resources made available for accreditation exercises are in many cases minimal.

Should it continue? This question, and related ones such as 'should this service be closed down?', or 'should the program be introduced to all schools in the county?' may be the one highlighted by the sponsor of the evaluation. An answer to this question will effectively call for your seeking evidence on some of the other questions in this list. What would count as persuasive evidence will need to be established through discussion. When this type of question is on the agenda, which is potentially job and career threatening for those involved in the program, ethical considerations loom large (see Chapter 3). Although, as argued in that chapter, it is a good working assumption that no evaluation is without an ethical dimension.

How can it be improved? Improvement is often the central question for new or innovatory programs or services. This is particularly so when it is feasible to run a 'pilot' version, perhaps before committing major resources to it. Here the evaluation is designed as part of the development of the program. However, even with well established and apparently successful programs or services, the question will almost always be of importance and concern for those involved. Suggestions for improvement will be particularly welcome when a program is in difficulties. Making sure program staff and others know this question is on the agenda also has the advantage of encouraging positive attitudes to the evaluation.

Types of Evaluation

Evaluations can be categorized in many different ways but a simple typology based on *needs, processes, outcomes* and *efficiency* is useful in designing evaluations to cover the questions raised in the previous section.

Evaluation of needs. When used to plan a new program, service or intervention, this is called *needs analysis.* It is not in itself an approach to program evaluation as at this stage there is no program to evaluate. However, as those carrying out small-scale evaluations may well be called upon to carry out this kind of exercise, an introduction to the topic is provided as Appendix A.

A study of the extent to which the needs of the target group are met when the program is actually running, sometimes referred to as a 'needs-based' evaluation, is effectively a type of process evaluation (where there is an attempt to assess whether what goes on when the program is in operation meets clients' needs) or, possibly, of outcome evaluation (where the concern is whether clients achieve desired outcomes).

Evaluation of processes. An analysis of what happens when the program is actually working. How is it being implemented? Does it operate as planned and expected? Who takes part in the program?

Evaluation of outcomes. If it appears a program is being implemented as planned, then it becomes reasonable to ask what kind of effect or impact the program is having on those taking part.

Evaluation of efficiency. If there is evidence a program or service is having a beneficial effect on participants, then it may be appropriate to go on to consider how these benefits compare with the costs incurred in running the program. If it gives equivalent results to lengthier and more expensive programs, it is a better use of resources.

The specialist nature of assessing costs and benefits, which extends into the realms of accountancy and economics, precludes an adequate treatment in a short general text like this. Some indication of what is involved, together with references to fuller treatments, is given as Appendix B.

Relations between evaluation of needs, processes, outcomes and efficiency. As Posovac and Carey (1997, p. 10) point out, there is a logical sequence to these four types of evaluation: '... without measuring need, planning cannot be rational; without effective implementation, good outcomes cannot be expected; and without achieving good outcomes, there is no reason to worry about efficiency'. This emphasizes that a focus on issues later in the sequence may be premature if earlier aspects have not been adequately attended to. So, an evaluation which shows problematic outcomes, perhaps that the program's goals have not been achieved, could be reflecting a lack of any proper implementation of the program or even that there was no need for it in the first instance.

These four types of evaluation link to the nine questions discussed in the previous section as illustrated in Figure 4.2. For each of the questions, an attempt is made to indicate the approaches likely to be relevant. However, each type may be relevant to several other questions. For example, the question 'does what is provided meet client needs?' clearly calls for some assessment of what those needs are. It could also depend on the nature of the outcomes for these clients, and on what actually happens to clients (i.e. the processes taking place). Similarly an evalua-

---

1) *What is needed?* Needs approach central (in relation to proposed program).

2) *Does what is provided meet client needs?* Needs approach central (in relation to current program). Evaluation of processes, outcomes and efficiency could all be relevant.

3) *What happens when it is in operation?* Processes approach central. Evaluation of needs could be relevant.

4) *Does it attain its goals or objectives?* Outcomes approach central. Evaluation of efficiency could be relevant.

5) *What are its outcomes?* Outcomes approach central. Evaluation of efficiency could be relevant.

6) *How do costs and benefits compare?* Efficiency approach central. Evaluation of outcomes is relevant.

7) *Does it meet required standards?* Any or all of the approaches could be relevant depending on circumstances.

8) *Should it continue?* Any or all of the approaches could be relevant depending on circumstances.

9) *How can it be improved?* Process approach likely to be central, but any or all of the approaches could be relevant depending on circumstances.

Figure 4.2: *Approaches to Evaluation Linked to the Questions in Figure 4.1*

tion of the benefits to these clients relative to the costs involved (i.e. an efficiency analysis) is also relevant to the question.

The figure also illustrates that whereas the first question, 'what is needed?' is only covered by an evaluation of needs, the other questions link in to more than one of the approaches.

For a new program, it may be that the chief evaluative effort goes into suggesting ways in which it might be developed and improved. This is likely to be based on documenting what is happening when the program is running (process focus). A more ambitious evaluation might still concentrate on improvement and the processes involved but widen the scope to seek answers to whether clients' needs are being met. Decisions on whether to continue the program might be based on the outcomes, perhaps particularly on whether planned goals are being reached. In other circumstances it might be adequate for a decision to be made about the continuation of the program on the basis of an evaluation of processes which reveals that planned activities were taking place.

An already-running program might have an evaluation limited solely to monitoring the processes taking place when it is in operation, or to a study of its outcomes. Or some combination of process and outcome evaluation might be attempted to cover a wider range of questions. If the program is considered to be in a definitive form, then the question of improvement might not be on the agenda. However, even well established programs are likely to benefit from considering what changes might be made, if only because aspects of the context in which they operate may have changed.

The temptation is to try to cover a wide range of questions. With necessarily limited resources this runs the risk none of them get dealt with adequately. Generally it is preferable to be more focused and to design the evaluation to obtain high-quality information about the really key question. When that has been done, it is worth while considering if and how data relevant to other, subsidiary, questions might be secured within the resources available.

Formative v. Summative Evaluation

The distinction between formative and summative evaluation, first made by Scriven (1967), is a useful one as it links to substantial differences in the design of evaluations. It is also useful in that it is one aspect of evaluation jargon which is widely understood and hence communicates well to a wide variety of audiences.

Formative evaluation. This is an evaluation where the main concern is to 'form' or develop the program. It is typically focused on a new program, often where the goal of the program is known and the purpose of the evaluation is to shape the program so as to help achieve that goal. Patton (1994) prefers to use the term 'developmental evaluation' rather than formative evaluation in situations where the ultimate goal of a program is not known. For him developmental evaluation is part of the process of developing goals and implementation strategies.

In practice, formative evaluations tend to raise very similar design issues to process evaluations. While a process evaluation could simply focus on what is happening with no intention to seek improvement, the main focus for a formative evaluation will usually be on process, i.e. what is actually going on in the program.

Summative evaluation. Here the intention is to provide an 'end-of-term report' indicating what the program has achieved. It is likely to focus on the outcomes of the program, including whether or not goals have been achieved. However, it could also deal with matters such as the implementation or otherwise of program plans, and whether or not the target population was reached, and their needs met.

Cronbach (1982, p. 12) has made the point that while the distinction between summative and formative evaluation is convenient, it suggests a false division into two classes. In particular it is quite feasible for an evaluation focusing on outcomes to be used formatively. When there are disappointing results one wants to know why there was a failure and how to do better next time. Even with successful results it may be that some aspects could and should be changed to make it work better. Also it is likely there would be a wish to use a successful program in some other context or setting. To do this in a principled way calls for an understanding of the reasons for success and the conditions under which it is likely to be repeated. This can be thought of as testing and, if necessary, changing the program theory. As Mohr (1995, p. 33) points out, following Chen (1990) and Judd and Kenny (1981), 'information on the mechanisms by which a treatment has its impact can be useful in the analysis of the generalization of the results, that is, in applying the program to different populations or to similar populations in other settings'. This claim is returned to later in the chapter, where the role of theory in the improvement of programs is discussed in some detail.

In practice it is rare to find either a purely formative or purely summative evaluation. Most providers of programs would like at least some information both about how they might improve the program, and also what kind of effects it has. Nevertheless you are likely to have the major emphasis on one or the other. Understanding the different emphases of the two approaches, summarized in Table 4.1, will assist you in building into your design the features necessary to work in either a formative or a summative mode.

Weiss (1998, p. 32) makes the useful point that while there are strong similarities between the formative-summative distinction and the process-outcome one, the terms have quite different implications. Formative and summative refer to the evaluator's intentions when undertaking the study, either to help develop the program, or to come to a judgement about it. Process and outcome, on the other hand, have nothing to do with the evaluator's intention but are concerned with the phase of the program which is focused on. Process deals with what goes

Table 4.1 *Emphases in formative and summative evaluations*

	Formative	Summative
Main evaluation approach	Evaluation of processes	Evaluation of outcomes
Main audience	Program team	Policy/decision-makers Sponsors
Main tasks	Clarifying goals Gathering information on program processes and implementation, problems and progress	Documenting outcomes and implementation
Methodology	Typically mainly qualitative	Typically mainly quantitative
Data collection	Ongoing	Usually mainly towards the end
Reporting	Several occasions, mainly through meetings and discussions Emphasis on suggestions for change and development	Formal written report at end Emphasis on outcomes and their implications
Your credibility depends on	Demonstrated understanding of program and rapport with team	Technical competence and impartiality

Source: Adapted and abridged from Herman *et al.* (1987, p. 26).

on during the program, outcome with the consequences for participants at the end.

Improvement as The Focus for Evaluation

The term 'formative' tends to carry with it the notion that it is most appropriate for a program or service which is in an early, unformed, state. Thinking in terms of 'improvement', while somewhat similar, applies in virtually all evaluation situations. As Posovac and Carey (1997, p. 26) point out 'Improvements can be made in programs when discrepancies are noted between what is observed and what was planned, projected, or needed'.

These discrepancies can be of many kinds, different ones being highlighted by different evaluation approaches. There may be discrepancies between the needs of the target clients and the plans and intentions of those proposing a program. Or discrepancies between the intended clients and those actually attending the program. Discrepancies can also occur between the planned program and that which is implemented. The intended outcomes may differ from those achieved. Seeking ways of reducing or eliminating such discrepancies provides a focus for the improvement of programs. Thinking in terms of discrepancies between the 'good' and the actual does carry the risk of reinforcing the stereotype that evaluators are simply concerned with criticizing. However, the message can be got across that nothing is ever perfect, and that we are working together in the positive business of improvement.

One way in which this can be done is by doing essentially the same thing as in outcome evaluation but, instead of simply assessing outcomes at the end of the process, doing this periodically. Relatively simple indicators of performance and progress can be used to provide feedback to program personnel. Good interim performance suggests they are on the right line, poor performance they should in some way adjust their activities. These may be thought of as intermediate goals or objectives.

However, the performance figures in themselves do not suggest directly what could or should be changed. This is where a theory of the operation of the program which helps to understand the reasons for success and the conditions under which it might be expected to occur, as discussed in the previous section, is of direct value.

Design Strategies

Knowing the general approach, or approaches, you need to take in an evaluation to get answers to the questions of interest helps in sorting out a design. While there are strong traditions of research design in the social sciences which program evaluators have drawn upon, a commonsense approach to the task can generate serviceable designs for small-scale evaluations.

This suggestion perhaps needs some qualification. I am not advocating a Luddite dismissal of the undoubted expertise social scientists can bring to bear on design issues. The ability to think like a social scientist, whether or not gained from a formal training in those disciplines, will stand you in good stead – see Pettigrew (1996) and Becker (1998) for stimulating discussions about what this involves. The argument is more that the constraints and particular features of designing small-scale evaluations are such that you are going to have to think the design task through for yourself and can't, as it were, easily pick up a design 'off the shelf'.

Constraints. These are mainly practical deriving from the limited time and resources you are likely to have at your disposal. Chapter 6 is largely devoted to emphasizing these practicalities. It is based on the confident assertion that it is better to deliver with a very simple do-able design than to get part way through a complex and methodologically sophisticated evaluation. There are also constraints in that, as discussed in the previous chapter, you as evaluator do not (or should not) have sole control of the design agenda. For good reasons, including increasing the likely use and usefulness of the evaluation, other 'stakeholders' have a voice.

Processes and Outcomes

In practice a large proportion of small-scale evaluations can be typified as focusing on either processes or outcomes. Or both. They are very different from each other and the following sections try to draw out their particular features. Hiving off needs analysis and efficiency evaluations to appendices reflects their relatively specialized nature and helps simplify the terrain. It will be pretty clear to you if you are being called on to carry out one or other of them and study of the appendix material, with the further reading indicated there, should help.

A note on evaluation of needs. If the question about whether a currently running program meets clients' needs is of importance to your sponsor or other stakeholders, the methods discussed in Appendix A can be adapted to provide relevant information.

Evaluation of Outcomes

Evaluation of the outcomes of programs is a frequently requested evaluative task. It comes under different guises including product evaluation, effectiveness evaluation and impact evaluation. The basic notion is that, with virtually all programs, something is supposed to change as a result of the program and outcome evaluations seek to assess whether or not this has happened.

Outcome evaluations tend to be quantitative. The evidence which many find most acceptable about outcomes is in numerical form. It is not too difficult to find something to measure which could be a possible outcome of a program. The task of selection is simplified if the goals or objectives of the program have been specified. However, even when this is the case, it may well be there are other unintended and unthought-of outcomes. Insight into what these might be can be provided by a prior process evaluation. The close involvement with the program process evaluation calls for is likely to reveal what is happening and any unforeseen consequences. For example, formal assessment of reading skills in the early years of schooling may be used to assess whether an objective of a newly instituted 'literacy hour' has been achieved. Classroom observation of consequent changes in day-to-day practices (perhaps a reduction in time spent on art, music and other creative activities) may suggest attention to other outcomes.

It is by no means essential for there to be a formal process evaluation to come up with likely outcomes. The methods of observation and discussions, possibly interviews with staff and administrators, which form a major part of process evaluations, can be used informally to provide suggestions.

Selection of a few outcome measures to target is the (relatively) easy part. Unfortunately there are both practical and theoretical problems likely to be encountered when dealing with outcomes. One practical difficulty is that many evaluations show equivocal outcomes. Average changes in the desired direction may be non-existent or, at best, disappointingly small. Theoretical, or methodological, difficulties start to arise when one wants to move from simply saying there has been a change, to claiming the change can be attributable to the program itself and not to some other cause.

Equivocal Nature of Evaluation Outcomes

Many evaluations of social programs show outcomes suggesting there has been little effect of the program on those taking part. Examples include various drug prevention programs (Gorman, 1998) and programs seeking to address early school failure (Jones et al., 1997). There are many possible explanations. Social programs, innovations, interventions and services are very complex things often dealing with difficult, sometimes intractable, problems. People themselves are notoriously complex. The contexts within which the programs are set vary widely which may influence outcomes. Program staff themselves, even when apparently faithfully implementing planned programs, may be differentially effective. Some of the difficulties may be in the hands of the evaluation and the evaluator, for example the outcome measures chosen may not be appropriate.

It has recently been suggested that a major difficulty arises from shortcomings in evaluation designs (Pawson and Tilley, 1997). They point out that instead of following the usual practice of looking at the overall or average effect of a program or intervention considered as an undifferentiated whole, it is much more productive to ask the question 'what works for whom under what circumstances?' In other words, they emphasize what is already known to most people who have been involved in evaluations – the program works best for some people and may well not work at all for others. Similarly there are some contexts and aspects of the program which seem favourable, and which are associated with particularly positive outcomes with some groups of clients. This approach to the design of evaluations is discussed in more detail later in the chapter.

Traditional Designs for Outcome Evaluations

The following subsections cover a range of traditional designs and indicate some of the difficulties in their use, together with an indication of the particular circumstances where they may be worth consideration.

In their simplest form, outcome evaluations look at the performance on completion of a program, on one or more measures, of clients who have taken part. A single 'output' measure by itself gives no indication of the possible improvement that has taken place. Somewhat more complex designs take measures both before and after involvement with the program which can obviously give a measure of possible change. However, such single-group designs are not equipped to answer questions about whether the program itself was responsible for the improvement seen. To do this, it is necessary to get involved with issues of experimental design.

Single-group outcome evaluation designs – post-test only. This is the simplest form of outcome design. In itself it provides no comparative information and usually needs to be supplemented in some way if it is to be useful. As this may be the only feasible outcome measure in many small-scale evaluations, it is returned to in the section 'Keeping it simple' after consideration of traditional designs.

Single-group outcome evaluation designs – pretest/post-test. It may be necessary to know if clients improved when taking part in the program. If so, the design has to be complicated by including testing both before and after. A weight-reduction program does not convince simply by producing post-program weights. This is a widely used outcome design in small-scale evaluations. It calls for a measure which can be used on successive occasions without problems. With some kinds of measure, such as taking a test of knowledge, the simple fact of having already taken the test will affect any second test irrespective of the nature or even existence of an intervening program.

If an improvement can be demonstrated, the next issue becomes whether the change is sufficiently large for notice to be taken of it. The traditional approach is to assess the statistical significance of the change from pretest to post-test. In statisticians' jargon a 'significant' result is simply one which is unlikely to have happened purely by chance. It is not necessarily 'significant' in the usual sense of the word, that is of importance or relevance.

The danger is of seeking to use this design to answer questions about whether the program actually *caused* the improvement. There are many other possible interpretations which are discussed below (see Figure 4.5).

Experimental and quasi-experimental outcome evaluation designs. Experimental designs are of many different types. In their simplest form they involve comparisons between an experimental group and a control group. The experimental group follow the program to be evaluated; the control group don't. Comparisons are made between the performance of the experimental and control groups after the program. Or sometimes the change in performance before and after the program is compared in the two groups. Figure 4.3 shows this in diagrammatic form. In a 'true' experimental design the participants are randomly assigned to the two groups. If this is done, then superior performance by the experimental group, which is unlikely statistically to have happened by chance, can be

	Before		After
Experimental group	O	X	O
Control group	O		O

Where O is a measure of performance and X is the program.
Participants are randomly assigned to experimental and control groups.

Figure 4.3 *Simple 'true' experimental design*

attributed to the effects of the program. The experimental method also calls for the control of other possible features ('variables') which might affect performance to increase the sensitivity of the comparison. For example, an evaluation of an innovatory educational program might control for previous educational or socioeconomic background of participants, perhaps restricting involvement to those with particular backgrounds. Robson (1994) discusses the logic of experimentation and covers a range of simple designs.

This style of investigation is widely used in experimental psychology and in some areas of medical and health research and evaluation. It derives from agricultural research where, for example, random allocation of some plots to receive a fertilizer and others to receive none is used to evaluate the effect of the fertilizer on plant growth. The strength of the experimental approach is in its ability to assess causal relationships. If the prescriptions of the approach are followed, in particular the use of random allocation of participants to the experimental and control conditions, then a 'statistically significant' result (i.e. a difference in favour of the experimental group which it is improbable by chance) can be attributed to the effects of the program. Early studies in program evaluation sought to follow this approach and it still has staunch advocates who regard 'randomized controlled trials' (RCT studies) as the 'gold standard' of evaluation (Sheldon, 1986; Oakley and Fullerton, 1996). However, it has come under severe attack for both practical and more fundamental reasons, some of which are indicated in Figure 4.4.

1) *Randomized allocation to experimental and control groups may not be **feasible**.* The evaluator may not be able to achieve this. Perhaps existing groups are to be used making a change in allocation impossible.
2) *Randomized allocation to experimental and control groups may not be **ethically permissible**.* Perhaps the intervention or service is a statutory right; or its denial to the control group otherwise considered unethical. Even if ethically justifiable it may be politically unacceptable.
3) *A no-treatment control group may not be possible.* The whole notion of 'no treatment' is very problematic when working with people. The 'placebo' (the sugar pill instead of the active drug) used in medical research can have complex effects.
4) *They are largely restricted to assessing whether programs have achieved one or at most a small number of stated objectives.* If you are interested in some of the other evaluation questions listed in Figure 4.1 experimental designs are not helpful. While it would be possible to focus on outcomes other than the objectives it would be necessary to prespecify them.
5) *They derive from a positivist methodology and the scientific tradition.* This implies abstraction of the units studied from their context; reduction to simple cause–effect relationships; and a view of the evaluator as exerting control, not only in setting up the groups but also of other variables which might affect the outcome. This will be seen as problematic by those who consider that social phenomena within open systems can't be equated with natural phenomena and natural science approaches.

Figure 4.4 Problems with the use of 'true' experimental designs in small-scale evaluations

An experimental design has to be accurately prespecified and the specification kept to. There is very little leeway for modification and this rigorous specification can cause problems in evaluations. The use of rigorous designs is likely to cause difficulties in carrying out the study. Those involved, both administrators and participants, may resist or try to subvert the rigid prescriptions called for by the design. If participants drop out during the evaluation, this may cause severe analysis problems.

Practical and ethical problems associated with randomized allocation can be mitigated by the use of *quasi-experimental designs*. The difference from 'true' experiments is that while all other features of the experimental approach are retained, some procedure other than randomization is employed. Campbell and Stanley (1966) introduced this notion and developed some of the issues in using such designs. For further development see Cook and Campbell (1979). The approach has been widely used in some areas of applied social science where 'field' conditions make the use of randomization impracticable. Unfortunately the logic of inferring cauzation is more complex than with true experiments. It depends on assessing possible *threats to internal validity*. Internal validity refers to the apparent effects of the program actually being due to the program, and not to other extraneous features. Figure 4.5 gives a list of possible threats, i.e. of things other than the program which might be responsible for the effects seen. The logic of randomization goes a long way towards nullifying the effects of such threats in true experiments. However, the specifics of each quasi-experiment, and of the pattern of results obtained in each one, have to be considered. The issue is whether or not each of these potential threats is an actual one for that evaluation.

An exercise of thinking in terms of possible threats to internal validity is more widely useful than simply for quasi-experimental outcome evaluations. It can be employed with advantage both in the design and the interpretation stage of many evaluation studies.

The problem of a no-treatment control can be dealt with by using comparison groups with different treatments, or different versions of the program. This design precludes any kind of absolute measure of the effects of the program but does permit an assessment of the relative effectiveness of the different conditions.

It is, of course, possible to combine the experimental approach to outcome evaluation with other approaches such as process evaluation. The philosophical and methodological underpinnings of the experimental approach, whether in its 'true' or 'quasi' variant, cause fundamental problems for some, leading to an effective veto on its use. As already indicated, others take the extreme opposite position of advocating randomized control trials as the only worthwhile approach to the assessment of the effectiveness of a program. A more pragmatic view is advocated here, with some of the considerations being indicated in Figure 4.6.

In practice, for many small-scale evaluations, it is unlikely that an experimental approach will be feasible. The formal establishment of experimental

1) *History.* Things that have changed in the participants' environments other than those forming a direct part of the enquiry (e.g. occurrence of major air disaster during study of effectiveness of desensitization programme on persons with fear of air travel).
2) *Testing.* Changes occurring as a result of practice and experience gained by participants on any pretests (e.g. asking opinions about factory farming of animals pre some intervention may lead respondents to think about the issues and develop more negative attitudes).
3) *Instrumentation.* Some aspect(s) of the way participants were measured changed between pretest and post-test (e.g. raters in an observational study using a wider or narrower definition of a particular behaviour as they get more familiar with the situation).
4) *Regression.* If participants are chosen because they are unusual or atypical (e.g. high scorers), later testing will tend to give less unusual scores ('regression to the mean'); e.g. an intervention program with pupils with learning difficulties where ten highest-scoring pupils in a special unit are matched with ten of the lowest-scoring pupils in a mainstream school – regression effects will tend to show the former performing relatively worse on a subsequent test.
5) *Mortality.* Participants dropping out of the study (e.g. in study of adult literacy programme – selective drop-out of those who are making little progress).
6) *Maturation.* Growth, change or development in participants unrelated to the treatment in the inquiry (e.g. evaluating extended athletics training programme with teenagers – intervening changes in height, weight and general maturity).
7) *Selection.* Initial differences between groups prior to involvement in the inquiry (e.g. through use of arbitrary non-random rule to produce two groups: ensures they differ in one respect which may correlate with others).
8) *Selection by maturation interaction.* Predisposition of groups to grow apart (or together if initially different); e.g. use of groups of boys and girls initially matched on physical strength in a study of a fitness programme.
9) *Ambiguity about causal direction.* Does A cause B, or B cause A? (e.g. in any correlational study, unless it is known that A precedes B, or *vice versa* – or some other logical analysis is possible).
10) *Diffusion of treatments.* When one group learns information or otherwise inadvertently receives aspects of a treatment intended only for a second group (e.g. in a quasi-experimental study of two classes in the same school).
11) *Compensatory equalization of treatments.* If one group receives 'special' treatment there will be organizational and other pressures for a control group to receive it (e.g. nurses in a hospital study may improve the treatment of a control group on grounds of fairness).
12) *Compensatory rivalry.* As above but an effect on the participants themselves (referred to as the 'John Henry' effect after the steel worker who killed himself through overexertion to prove his superiority to the new steam drill); e.g. when a group in an organization sees itself under threat from a planned change in another part of the organization and improves performance.

Figure 4.5   *Threats to internal validity*
Source: After Cook and Campbell (1979, pp. 51–5).

- *If* the question of whether the program achieves its objectives is key; and
- *if* it is important to demonstrate that the program actually caused these effects; and
- *if* it is feasible, and ethical, to set up experimental and control groups using random allocation;
- *then* consider including an experiment within your evaluation; and
- *if* random allocation is not possible but the other conditions apply, consider incorporating a quasi-experiment instead.

An experimental design is *particularly indicated*:

- *If* your sponsor, and/or other audiences you wish to influence, are positively inclined to experimental approaches and the quantitative statistical findings they generate.

Figure 4.6 *When might you use an experimental design?*

and control groups, or of contrasting groups, of sufficient size for statistical comparisons to be set up, and sufficiently isolated from each other for you to be reasonably sure they don't affect each other in some way, is difficult to achieve. Typically the study will take place in a single setting, or in settings which are geographically and socially close.

Practical Significance of Improvement

The practical or meaningful significance of an improvement following a program or intervention is not the same thing as statistical significance. The latter simply means the observed change is unlikely to have happened purely by chance. With an appropriate experimental design it is then possible to go further and assert this change is not only improbable as a chance occurrence but it can also be attributable to the program or intervention itself. While this is clearly of value, it says little or nothing about the importance of the change. This is sometimes referred to as the difference between statistical and 'clinical' significance. In clinical settings the knowledge that a treatment has statistically significant results (based upon group averages) does not necessarily imply it helps a particular patient. Similarly in evaluation there are no easy statistical approaches to assessing whether a change is sufficiently large to be meaningful. This value judgement is best undertaken through discussions with relevant stakeholders.

Single-Case Experimental Designs for Outcome Evaluation

Experimental designs have been developed which, instead of using groups of various kinds, target the individual client; or indeed any other unit which can be conceptualised as a 'case' in the evaluation (e.g. a hospital ward or school class). Derived primarily from the work of the radical behaviourist B. F. Skinner (see Sidman, 1960) their individualized focus has an attraction in the context of small-scale evaluations. Single-case designs share a concern for outcomes with the other experimental designs but call for some type of indicator of outcome which can be measured repeatedly. Typically a series of measures is taken prior to the program or other intervention, and a further series after the intervention. Comparisons are intra-case with individual clients acting as their own control.

Many of the studies have a clinical focus, particularly in the field of behaviour modification where, say, the intention is to reduce the frequency of occurrence of some problem behaviour. A range of designs is available (see Robson, 1993, pp. 109–15) although those used in evaluation, largely restricted to the social work field, have tended to be simple (Sheldon, 1983, Thyer, 1993; Kazi, 1998a). If it is possible to select a reliable and valid outcome measure, which can be used repeatedly on a substantial number of occasions, then single-case designs avoid many of the practical problems in using experimental group designs for small-scale evaluations. However, similar philosophical and methodological issues can be raised. Indeed, in behaviour modification, there is an explicit equation between understanding a phenomenon and being able to predict and control its occurrence which disturbs many.

Experiment-Like Designs for Outcome Evaluations

Some evaluations share many of the characteristics, general approach and aspirations of experimental designs but lack their control over assignment to different conditions central to these designs. They tend to arise when there is an interest in the impact of a program, but this kind of selection has already taken place before the evaluator comes on the scene. Or there are other reasons why the evaluator cannot influence this process.

These designs are variously labelled as *ex post facto* (i.e. 'after the fact'), *correlational, historical* or *passive observation*. Mohr (1995, pp. 226–47) provides an insightful analysis of such designs. His conclusion is that their results are seldom persuasive and unambiguous. If of importance to policy they are likely to be doubted and disputed. Mohr's recommendation is that they should usually be avoided. He also suggests it may be possible to build within such a study some mini-studies which incorporate selection set up by the evaluator.

Keeping it Simple

While Mohr's points are well taken, they run the risk of outcome-based studies becoming an endangered species within small-scale evaluations. As previously stressed, resource considerations and other practical constraints can make it very difficult to set up adequate traditional experimental designs. However, it may be that for your particular situation a very simple type of design will suffice.

For example, the single-group post-test-only design is a common form of outcome design in small-scale evaluations. Suppose a program is devised to help people who do not use aeroplanes because of a fear of flying. The outcome measure might be the proportion of clients who take advantage of a free flight offer in the month following the program. The knowledge that 90% of them take up the offer could reasonably be viewed as an adequate indication of the success of the program. For some audiences this would constitute a convincing outcome measure.

For other audiences it might be necessary to support this finding in some way before it becomes convincing. An implicit comparison of some kind might be made. Perhaps it is known from the background of those on the program that it would be highly unlikely any of them would have accepted the offer without having been involved. In many evaluations it is possible to collect additional information, often about processes, which can lend support. More generally, information about outcomes which might be judged inadequate or unconvincing by itself helps to round out the picture produced from a process evaluation.

Methods Used in Outcome Evaluations

In outcome evaluations the task is much more the selection of appropriate outcome measures than of the use of particular research methods. Such measures will be specific to particular programs. Thus, for example, a program for remedial writing in a school or college context might use as an outcome measure the assessment of a written essay. Or, more indirectly, some test of knowledge of written expression. Programs for men showing violence to women would be likely to focus on the prevalence and frequency of their violence and other aspects thought to be associated with it, such as controlling and coercive behaviour.

When the program has clear objectives, and this is a main focus of the evaluation, the outcome to be measured is clear. How the measurement is actually done can remain problematic. A program training communication skills may have as its objective an increase in communicated empathy. An appropriate measure for this could well be a matter of some debate (Nerdrum, 1997). For a program on stopping smoking it is pretty clear what one wishes to measure, though there may be difficulties in getting reliable and valid data. If self-report is used, then data may reflect the clients' wish to please or to prove their own abilities, rather than actually represent post-program smoking levels.

Evaluation of Processes

The first approaches to evaluation focused on the summative measurement of outcomes. Experimental and quasi-experimental designs using the statistical analysis of quantitative data were employed. The program itself was not studied directly. The assumption was made that because the program developers said it worked in a particular way, this was actually what happened. However, it rapidly became clear this was a very questionable assumption. Pioneers in the field such as Ralph Tyler (1942/1991) found few places where programs actually operated as planned.

This provided one stimulus for the development of evaluations of program processes. Checking on whether planned programs are being delivered is important in its own right, as well as a sensible precursor to establishing the effectiveness of a program in outcome terms. There are other potential evaluation questions directly to do with process, including:

- How are clients brought into the program?
- What happens to them when involved with the program?
- Are clients' needs being met?
- How do staff and clients interact?
- How is the program perceived by staff and clients?
- What is the day-to-day reality of the program?
- What are the patterns of activity (including both formal and informal, unanticipated activities)?
- Is the program changing? If so, how?

Answers to these questions can provide direct help in improving the way in which programs run, that is, in their implementation. Process information can also help in understanding outcome data, again providing pointers to the improvement of the program. Inevitably some clients will have more favourable outcomes than others. Some of the settings in which it runs may be more effective than others. There is likely to be similar variability between program staff either on an individual or a group basis. Detailed knowledge about what is happening helps to disentangle these effects. Some will be linked to the quality of the program provided. Particularly successful clients may have had excellent staff, or be in favourable settings. All this is valuable in helping to specify the conditions under which the program works best.

As well as improving implementation, detailed information on whom the program works best for, and in which contexts it is particularly effective, can be of assistance in understanding why the program works. Knowledge of these underlying mechanisms provides a powerful tool for improving the program itself. This type of analysis is discussed in the section below on 'Evaluating for improvement'.

Qualitative or Quantitative Data Collection?

The evaluation of program processes typically relies primarily on qualitative data collection. Observation and interviewing (often of an informal type) are commonly used, together with the analysis of existing data such as program materials and records of meetings. This appears to many evaluators to be the most appropriate way of capturing the complex and fluid stream of events taking place when even a very simple program involving people takes place.

However, the opportunity to collect quantitative data which may help in describing how the program is operating should be investigated. Relatively simple measures of aspects such as attendance patterns, or frequency and length of sessions, not only help to describe the reality of the program, but can also provide possible links to outcomes. Figure 4.7 suggests some possible indicators.

The extent to which a program can be captured by measurement of a limited set of variables such as these will vary very much from program to program. It is easier with a well established and fully specified program where appropriate measures should be relatively easy to select, based on preliminary observation and/or discussions with program staff. For new programs, especially those which are at a developmental stage, this may not be feasible. Observational and other qualitative data can be collected from such programs in the first instance. Analysis of this should help in selecting possible variables.

While most of the attributes on Weiss's list are easy to assess and measure, the notion of 'quality of service' (and indeed 'quality' in general) is much more problematic. It is neither sensible nor feasible for most evaluators to make judgements about the quality of performance of professionals and practitioners. They are unlikely to have the specific expertise or credibility to do this. However, quality of provision may be central to the effectiveness of a program. A well planned program can obviously fail because it is poorly delivered. One way forward is to use accepted performance indices which are in themselves factual and non-controversial. Thus client-practitioner ratios or measures of resource provision might be viewed as acceptable as, at least partial, proxies for quality in some situations.

If it is considered essential to assess quality directly, the development of appropriate measures will take considerable time and effort. It is likely to involve the development of a rating scale; the training of people in its use; and demonstrating high interobserver agreement (i.e. showing that different people use the scale in essentially the same way). However, it is unlikely that a small-scale evaluation will be able to devote the necessary resources to do this. There is considerable interest in the assessment of quality in many professional contexts. For example Bickman amd Salzer (1997) discusses quality in the context of mental health services, as an introduction to a journal issue on quality and the future of quality measurement. You may be able to find an already-existing instrument which appears appropriate. It will still be necessary for raters to be

1)	Type of programmatic activity.
2)	Characteristics of staff offering the service.
3)	Frequency of service (strength of treatment).
4)	Duration of service.
5)	Intensity (dosage).
6)	Integrity of service to intended (planned) design.
7)	Size of group receiving service.
8)	Stability of activity (vs. frequent shift in focus).
9)	Quality of service.
10)	Responsiveness to individual needs.

Figure 4.7 *Indicators of program processes*
Source: From Weiss (1998, p. 130).

trained in its use and for interobserver agreement to be established.

Caution about stepping into this 'quality' field is necessary because of its extreme sensitivity. Continuing controversy about its assessment in UK schools in part arises because of the political context of league tables of schools with, at the extreme, 'shaming and blaming' of the failures. The perceived amateur nature of the quality judgements made by inspection teams does not help.

Program Monitoring

Monitoring is usually taken to be the routine activities undertaken by program management or staff to keep track of the way in which it is working. These activities may be a central requirement in an organization. Perhaps all constituent parts of the organization, including the program, are required to report and retain information to some standardized format. Or it may be a one-off so that particular records relevant to the progress of the program are maintained. Commonly there is a fixed timetable of reporting dates, perhaps annually at the end of a calendar or financial year.

Clearly there is potential overlap between the data collected for monitoring purposes and that for an evaluation, primarily but not necessarily exclusively for process evaluations. It has not been unknown for staff responsible for monitoring and those running an evaluation to be collecting the same information, and for there to be conflict between the two groups. This is particularly so when outside evaluators prize their independence and objectivity, and internal staff want to present 'their' program in the best possible light.

The stance taken here (as elaborated in Chapter 2) has been that even for an outside evaluator there is great advantage in working collaboratively and co-operatively with program staff of various kinds. Exploring ways of increasing convergence between monitoring and evaluative information can deliver dividends. Evaluators may well be able to use monitoring data and/or persuade those doing the monitoring either to modify or add to the information they collect. Perhaps the timescale of the two activities can be harmonized so that the data are available in time for both purposes. An added bonus is likely to be that the evaluator gets to appreciate the program from the perspective of the monitoring staff. They get to understand about the evaluation, and possibly become more identified with it.

Computer-based management information systems (MIS) are becoming increasingly used and increasingly sophisticated. They may well contain much process information, including detailed data on the progress of individual clients, useful for evaluative purposes. Indeed there is much to be said for maintaining a single common database of this kind which can be used for both monitoring and evaluation. It is highly desirable for an exploration of possibilities of this kind to take place as soon as the design of the evaluation becomes reasonably clear.

There are problems both in the use of MISs, and the use of monitoring data more generally. They are essentially those arising from data being collected for some purpose other than evaluation, and the points made about the use of such data in Chapter 5 apply. You have to consider whether this initial use will have led to biases in the way it is recorded. Much of the monitoring data appears on the surface at least, to be quite factual and not likely to be prone to distortion, but the possibility of bias should be seriously considered. For example, attendance rates at schools might well be over-reported if truancy is being used as an index of the success or otherwise of a school.

A more general problem can arise from monitoring records being completed in a perfunctory manner. It is not uncommon to find situations in human service organizations where there is considerable resistance to computerized systems. Practitioners may regard the entry of data into such systems as a low-priority task which can be completed when the pressure of work slackens, hence reducing its accuracy and quality.

Finally, ethical problems may arise when data are collected for monitoring purposes and subsequently used for an evaluation. The general guidelines presented in Chapter 3 apply. The solution is to ensure you have fully informed consent to gaining access to any such data, and that other aspects such as anonymity and confidentiality are guaranteed. There could be implications for those involved with monitoring. They may need to give further consideration to the ethical implications of their own work.

Rossi and Freeman (1993, Chap. 4) provide a detailed account of the contribution that program monitoring can make to evaluation. They make the point that monitoring is directed at three key questions:

- The extent to which a program is reaching the appropriate target population.
- Whether or not its delivery of services is consistent with program design specification.
- What resources are being or have been expended in the conduct of the program.

These are all questions likely to be of interest in evaluations.

Insiders and Reactivity

In many evaluations of processes, the evaluator is an insider. Either she is an actual member of the program team already, or effectively seeks to become a member of the team – albeit with a distinctive role. While the prime role is that of evaluator, it commonly also extends to an involvement in the design and running of the program. The role can extend into the evaluator also acting as an advocate for the program in meetings and discussions. It has also been argued in Chapter 2 that there is advantage in an outside evaluator abandoning the detached outsider role and working together with program staff in a more collaborative fashion.

All this can cause problems in compromising the objectivity of the evaluator (McDonald, 1976) and there is the likelihood of reactivity. In other words the presence of an evaluator may in itself affect the working of the program. However, as Pole (1993, pp. 111–12) points out, this effect may well be for the better and could actually ' encourage participants to step back to take a critical look at what they are doing. Contamination does inevitably occur but the evaluator must seek to make it positive contamination.' It should be borne in mind that there can be reactivity problems even in situations where the evaluator is impeccably objective and distant from the program. For example, the requirement to complete a formal test as part of an outcome evaluation may well affect the operation of a program, particularly when ethical considerations call for those involved having prior notice that testing will take place. Here it is the test instrument itself which may cause interference with running of the program (again, possibly, but not necessarily, for the better!). It could be argued that, when the evaluator has been 'part of the furniture' for some time in a process evaluation, observation of program activities and informal interviews with those involved will be less intrusive than such formal testing.

New Programs

Process evaluations can take place in the early stages of the development of a program or service, when they have a primarily formative role. It is likely that at this stage there will be piloting of all or parts of the program. Perhaps alternative versions of different parts might be tried out, either at the same time or consecutively. It is when the program is in this initial fluid state that this formative evaluation is likely to be of greatest value.

Even quite simple evaluations can provide insight into the problems a program or intervention is likely to face and highlight possible ways of overcoming them. It is often the case that the evaluation of processes at an early stage for formative purposes is planned to be followed by some kind of outcome evaluation. Going beyond an exclusive focus on process at this early stage also provides the opportunity of testing out possible evaluation procedures and instruments for the later stage.

Methods Used in Process Evaluations

The main methods used in small-scale process evaluations are probably *observation* and/or *interviews* with staff, clients and program administrators, together with the examination of *existing documents and records*. Particular aspects of a process evaluation may call for other methods. For example an assessment of coverage, the extent to which the target population is reached, may be best approached by means of a sample *survey*. This could be mainly or exclusively using simple yes/no type questions which could be analysed quantitatively. Monitoring the extent to which the program meets specific requirements could be largely based on simple *checklists* recording whether or not certain features are present.

In general, however, process evaluations tend to be more fluid and unstructured than other types of evaluation and their quality relies largely upon your sensitivity and empathy to the situation and those involved, rather than on sophisticated methods of gathering data.

Combining Process and Outcome Approaches

The previous sections on evaluation of processes and outcomes provide pointers to the kinds of things to be considered when designing such evaluations. By now you should be developing a feel for the 'flavour' of your evaluation in relation to the relative emphasis you need to give to these aspects. Table 4.2 may help you to locate it in this respect. The study of processes is likely to tell you about implementation issues, giving pointers to ways in which the program can be improved. A 'pure' outcome study gives little help in this regard and, as improvement is rarely off the agenda, this provides a strong incentive to devote at least a small amount of time and attention to studying processes in a largely outcome-oriented study. Conversely it could be argued that a 'pure' process evaluation will suffice for those simply interested in the operation of the program (including those with an aversion to the collection of quantitative data usually linked to measuring outcomes). However, it is a rare sponsor who is not desirous of some outcome information and even for those with strong process leanings, it may well be worth while to devote some small amount of resources to collecting easily accessible outcome data.

The suggestion is made in Table 4.2 that not only should you go for a 'balanced' process/output design if both process and output are important to the questions you need to answer (hardly surprising!) but you should also do this if improvement is top of your agenda. The argument developed below is that to make principled suggestions for improvement, beyond obvious things like picking up on failures of implementation of the planned program, you need to understand how the program works. And to understand how it works, you need not only information about outcomes but also to be able to tie this in to process.

Evaluating for Improvement

The questions about programs we have previously considered (listed in Figure 4.1), while covering the most likely ones to be raised by sponsors and others involved with the program, have an important omission.

This is *Why does a program achieve its effects?* Or, put in other terms – How does it work? It is a question rarely highlighted by persons commissioning evaluations. Indeed, many evaluators would be surprised to see such questions posed. Seeking the underlying reasons for the effectiveness, or otherwise, of programs or services tends to be seen as at best an optional extra. It smacks of the theoretical, and theory tends to get a bad press. As Malcolm Scriven (1991, p. 360) puts it, theories are 'a luxury

Table 4.2 *Design priorities*

	Largely 'process' oriented	Broadly even handed between 'process' and 'outcomes'	Largely 'outcomes' oriented
Main interest in	What happens when the program is in operation	How the program can be improved	Outcomes, particularly program goals
Some interest in	Whether what is provided meets client needs	What happens when the program is in operation	Whether what is provided meets client needs
	and/or	and/or	and/or
	whether it meets required standards	outcomes, particularly program goals	whether it meets required standards
	and/or	and/or	and/or
	if it should continue.	whether what is provided meets client needs	if it should continue.
		and/or	
	It is assumed you will also have an interest in program improvement	whether it meets required standards	It is assumed you will also have an interest in program improvement
		and/or	
		if it should continue	

for the evaluator, since they are not even essential for explanations, and explanations are not essential for 99% of all evaluations'. One might think that even if explanations might be called for to round out some large fully researched evaluations, the small-scale evaluation is quintessentially within that 99%. However, following the lead of Pawson and Tilley (1997, p. 83) the position taken here is that Scriven is seriously misleading on this point. As Kurt Lewin (1951, p. 169) advised applied psychologists 'there is nothing so practical as a good theory'.

Program Theory

Theory can mean many things. We will take it here to refer to the assumptions, principles and hypotheses used both to develop programs or services and to understand their effects (Chen, 1990, p. 40). It appears reasonable that getting these assumptions, principles and hypotheses out into the open will help both in developing them, and in focusing the evaluation. This may in turn lead to a better understanding of the effect of the program and help in finding ways of increasing its effectiveness.

A program will have some kind of basis – an idea or hypothesis, to use a grander term, or probably a number of such ideas. Early AIDS prevention campaigns in the UK sought to instil fear of this dread disease with images and music designed to frighten. The underlying idea was that this would then make non-safe sex less likely. Similar anti-drugs campaigns relied on graphic images of gaunt heroin addicts.

These underlying ideas may or may not have been articulated and fully thought through by those involved in designing the program. However, once they have been explicitly stated, they help in designing the evaluation. Knowing that the idea is for a series of TV commercials with fear-inducing images and music which is intended to influence sexual activity helps in deciding how the evaluation is to be focused. The program designers may simply have asked evaluators whether exposure to the TV commercials decreases high-risk sexual activity. It is, of course, perfectly feasible to design an evaluation which tests whether they are effective in this way. The sad and dispiriting finding from a host of previous evaluation efforts is that overall effects, perhaps comparing an experimental group who view the commercials with a control group who don't, are typically very weak and inconsistent, and not uncommonly the reverse of what is expected.

However, understanding the ideas behind the program gives us additional purchase on the problem. This can go in several directions. We might question the idea itself. Does increasing fear actually have a predictable effect on what people do? This is an area well worked over by experimental psychologists. When emotions are involved, the effects seem very complex. Paradoxical outcomes, where the fear increases the 'kicks' in the situation, are not unknown. We can ask simple questions, such as whether the ads do actually arouse fear. There are suggestions that the emaciated images of heroin addicts, far from being aversive, were actually considered as positive role models by some young audiences, so-called 'heroin chic'. Knowledge of the idea or hypothesis then helps to take the lid off the 'black box' view suggested by sole concentration on input (TV commercial) and output (change in practices).

A theory doesn't have to be right. There could be a range of competing, and possibly complementary, theories underlying the operation of a program or service. There may well be other theories which help explain why the program will not achieve its objectives.

Theory-based evaluation has had several advocates (e.g. Chen, 1990; Weiss, 1995) but it is fair to say that it has not made much headway in evaluation circles. Weiss analyses both its potential contribution and proposes ways of overcoming obstacles in its use. As she says 'Programs are usually designed on the basis of experience, practice knowledge, and intuition, and practitioners go about their work without articulating the conceptual foundations of what they do' (1997, p. 503). The argument here is that, whether or not we refer to these bases for design or conceptual foundations as theories, they do exist, and there is advantage in getting them consciously articulated.

Using 'Realist' Language

'Realism' is a philosophical approach, which in early versions was casti-gated for its naivete. It has reappeared in more subtle forms, where it is perhaps most commonly known as 'scientific realism', to become an influential perspective in the philosophy of both natural and social science (Harré, 1972; Bhaskar, 1978; 1986; House, 1991; Sayer, 1992). In its modern guise, it seeks to counter the devastating criticisms that have been made of the traditional positivistic stance in science, and is com-monly characterised as 'postpositivistic'. In social science, it is currently in contention with postmodern and social constructionist or constructivist views for pole position. Blaikie (1993) provides an accessible introduc-tion to these debates. It has recently had an influence on evaluation, notably through the work of Pawson and Tilley (1997) who effectively provide a manifesto for its use in this field.

At a relatively superficial level, which does not necessarily call for strict adherence to the philosophical implications of scientific realism, a realist terminology gives a helpful way of thinking about both theory and the design stage of an evaluation. For scientific realists, theories are

Mechanism	Leading to	and	and	resulting in
Improved teacher understanding of home culture	Increased teacher sympathy with children and their view of the world	Teaching in terms comfortable and understandable to students	Increased student morale	
Increased parent understanding of school's expectations	Parental support and encouragement with child's homework and/or Parental support for better school attendance	Greater conscientiousness of work by students Improved school attendance		Increased achievement in reading
Identification of student's special problems (health, emotional, etc.)	Referral to sources of help in school or out	Student's receipt of special help	Improvement of health, emotional condition, etc.	

Figure 4.8 *Example of possible mechanisms (1): a program to improve students' achievement in reading through home visits by teachers (Weiss, 1972)*

Source: Adapted from Weiss (1998, p. 63).

	Mechanism	Leading to	and	and	resulting in
Program give patients something to do for themselves	Increased tolerance of aversive stimuli; decreased sensitivity to	Decreased treatment-seeking behaviour	Increased likelihood of patient, family and medical care staff perceiving the patient is well enough to go home symptoms		Increased probability of hastened discharge
	Decreased emotional stress	Decreased adrenal hormone	Decreased blood coagulation	Decreased probability of thrombosis	
			and/or		
			Increased immunologic response	Decreased probability of infection	

Figure 4.9 *Example of possible mechanisms (2): a program to help post-surgery patients recover more quickly and experience fewer side-effects*

Source: Based on Cook and Devine (1982), cited in Posovac and Carey (1997, 58–9).

proposals about how *mechanisms* operate in *contexts* to produce *outcomes*. Or, in other words proposals about why the program works, for whom and in what circumstances. Mechanisms are at the heart of this. Figures 4.8 and 4.9 give examples of mechanisms. In Weiss's study, one possible mechanism whereby the program might improve students' reading is through the teacher acquiring improved understanding of the home. However, she considers there are at least two other possible mechanisms. The figures also illustrate that the operation of a particular mechanism would have effects which might be picked up by study of the processes taking place, or through assessment of intermediate outcomes.

These mechanisms are not mutually exclusive. All or any of them might be operative and it may be that some work with some children, parents or teachers but not with others. Or perhaps they only work for some home backgrounds, particular types of school, etc. This illustrates the possible context-dependence of specific mechanisms. Pawson and Tilley (1997) analyse various mechanisms and contexts which might be relevant to the use of CCTV to reduce theft in a car park, as shown in Figure 4.10. This is only a selection from the set of possible mechanisms and contexts they put forward. Analysis of the detailed relationship between the introduction of the cameras in different car parks and related crime rates would provide evidence for the operation of different mechanisms in particular contexts.

Possible mechanisms: CCTV reduces crime by:	Which mechanism(s) fired depends on the context:
a) *The 'caught in the act' mechanism.* CCTV could reduce car crime by making it more likely that *present offenders* will be observed on screen, detected instantly and then arrested, removed, punished and deterred. b) *The 'you've been framed' mechanism.* CCTV could reduce car crime by deterring *potential offenders* who will not wish to risk investigation, apprehension and conviction by the evidence captured on videotape.	i) *The 'criminal clustering' context.* A given rate of car crime may result from widely differing prevalences of offending. For example if there are 1,000 incidents per annum, this may be by anything from a single (very busy) offender to as many as 1,000 offenders, or still more if they operate in groups. A mechanism leading to disablement of the offender (as in (a)) holds potential promise according to the offender–offence ratio. ii) *The 'lie of the land' context.* Cars parked in the CCTV blind spots in car parks will be more vulnerable if the mechanism is increased chances of apprehension through evidence on videotape (as in (b)).

Figure 4.10 *Example of mechanisms related to contexts: reduction of car park crime through use of closed-circuit TV cameras*

Source: From Pawson and Tilley (1997, pp. 78–80).

This analysis, while plausible, is largely conjectural and hypothetical. However their evaluation of a prison education program (Duguid and Pawson, 1998) is based on an actual detailed study, one aspect of which is presented as Figure 4.11 (see also Table 6.2). They contrast two context-mechanism-outcome patterns based upon the analysis of the performance of different subgroups of prisoners. This shows that while there are modest effects overall of the prison education program, two of these sub-groups perform particularly well in terms of their subsequent low reconviction levels. Their interpretation is that a 'disadvantaged' subgroup (prisoners with little or no previous education and with a growing string of convictions) who show modest levels of engagement and success with the program trigger a 'habilitation' process. This leads to the inmate experiencing self-realization and social acceptability for the first time and subsequent very low relative reconviction rates. A second 'career criminal' group (prisoners who have served the majority of their time in maximum security penitentiaries) who show both high levels of engagement and success with the program trigger a 'rehabilitation' process. Here the inmate experiences changes in powers of self-reflection and reasoning which also lead to very low relative reconviction rates.

This was a relatively large-scale study lasting several years for which this type of subgroup analysis is perhaps best fitted. Nevertheless, the basic ideas of thinking in terms of mechanisms and contexts to find out how the program operates can be applied widely. Practitioners, professionals and other program staff appear to find thinking in these terms about what underlies the effectiveness, or otherwise, of their practice provides them with a quickly accessible language (Kazi, 1998b; Pawson and Tilley, 1998).

Program Activities and Mechanisms

It is not the program activities themselves which constitute the mechanisms, but the response they generate in those involved. These activities are, of course, important. Program developers not only have theories (ideas, hunches) about possible mechanisms, they also assume that the various program activities lead to the operation of these mechanisms. Figure 4.12 gives an example. It illustrates that the staff involved with

Context		Mechanism		Outcome
'Disadvantaged' background	+	Habilitation process	=	Lowest level of reconviction compared with norm for such inmates
'Criminal' background	+	Rehabilitation process	=	Lowest level of reconviction compared with norm for such inmates

Figure 4.11 *Example of realist context–mechanism–outcome (CMO) analysis*

Source: From Pawson and Tilley (1997, p. 113).

Contexts	Possible mechanisms
Provision of training in accessible location; payment for attendance; day-care facilities	Regular attendance
Quality of training; match of training to market needs	Acquisition of useful skills
Expectation of good work habits; provision of help and support	Acquisition of appropriate job behaviours
Provision of job information	Job seeking
Existence of appropriate jobs	

Figure 4.12 *Relationship between contexts and mechanisms in a job training program*

Source: Derived from Weiss (1998, p. 59).

this program have assumed that a sequence such as providing good training in accessible locations, paying for attendance, providing child care, etc. (which are part activities and part contexts) is provided. Given their delivery, then the program theory suggests participants will make progress towards the goal of employment. Poor delivery makes such progress unlikely. So will poor attendance or inappropriate behaviour on a job. Setting out possible mechanisms of change linked to sequences of program activities provides pointers to what the evaluation might focus on. Evidence suggesting a breakdown in either sequence makes it possible to pinpoint where there is a problem. If the program achieves its objectives, then it is possible to explain how this came about.

Such neat and tidy preconceptualized sequences are unlikely to represent the reality of what you find when evaluating. Providing you allow flexibility in data collection you may well pick up very different sequences from those envisaged. Remember that unanticipated consequences are the rule rather than the exception in those necessarily complex interventions we know as social programs. Different mechanisms may be operating from those program developers thought; their ideas and hunches may have been wrong. But they, with your help, may be able to come up with better ones. Similarly the program activities may be very different from those planned. All this helps both in understanding program operation and getting a feel for where and how improvements might be made.

Mechanisms and Program Design

If you are in at the program design stage, then work done on coming up with a set of possible mechanisms and the contexts in which they are most likely to operate pushes the team towards decisions on:

• whom the program will focus on;
• where you will try it out;

- when is a good time to start; and
- what part of the program will be targeted first?

One strategy is to seek the optimal for each of these. That is, to set it up in the design of the program so you have the best possible situation to trigger the mechanism(s). Say early teen female smokers from non-smoking households, or late teen male smokers attending sports training sessions. An alternative is to seek to achieve a mixed bag where you design for the best chance of firing one or more of the mechanisms, together with incorporating situations where mechanisms are least likely to be triggered. If your analysis of possible mechanisms has some merit, then this will give differential patterns of results.

This latter approach bears a surface similarity to the traditional control group design (or more accurately a contrasting groups design where there are two or more differing 'experimental' conditions, rather than an experimental and a 'no-treatment' control group). The difference is that the traditional designs focus exclusively on pre–post differences (possibly combined with analyses of post-program differences for different conditions) and assess whether or not such differences are *statistically significant*. They tell you whether or not the differences are likely to have occurred by chance, but not why they occurred. The hypothesized mechanisms, however, are directly focused on the how and why of the operation of the program. There is potentially a wide set of corroborating and confirming evidence about the plausibility of mechanisms obtainable from both outcome and process data.

There may be substantial constraints on the focus of the program or intervention which preclude a free-ranging approach to 'who', 'where', etc. The money may only be available for a program in run-down housing estates or for interventions with particular groups. At the extreme, this can raise serious ethical issues. Discussions may reveal extreme pessimism about being able to come up with something that would improve a difficult situation; even perhaps a worry that it could be counterproductive and make it worse. Serious questions then need to be asked about the propriety of getting involved. However, given good will, energy and availability of resources, it is rare that, even with daunting constraints, something worth while cannot be mounted. And it is, of course, not surprising that the problems and issues for which intervention is considered necessary are seldom straightforward and simple of solution.

Mechanisms and Evaluation Questions

It has previously been suggested that the purpose or purposes of an evaluation help frame the questions to which you seek answers when carrying out the evaluation. Suggestions about possible mechanisms assist in developing these questions and in making them more specific. For example, in the program referred to in Figure 4.8, one obvious purpose will be to evaluate the extent to which the program leads to increased achievement in reading. A second purpose would most likely be to improve the effectiveness of the program itself. The possible mechanisms listed in the figure provide suggestions for further developing the set of evaluation questions. Thus to the question about outcomes:

- Does the program lead to increased achievement in reading?

might be added further questions, such as:

- Is student morale increased?
- Is there greater conscientiousness of work by students?
- Is school attendance improved?
- Is student health and emotional condition improved?

If these questions refer to the performance or condition of students on completion of the program, they are also possible outcome questions. It might also be possible to make intermediate assessments on some or all of these measures.

The possible mechanisms also help to focus questions about process. Thus answers to the questions:

- Do teachers following the program show increased sympathy with children and their view of the world? and
- Do teachers following the program teach in terms which are comfortable and understandable to students?

help to assess whether or not the 'increased teacher understanding of home culture' mechanism is in operation. Similarly, answers to:

- Do parents involved in the program give parental support and encouragement with their child's homework? and
- Do parents involved in the program give parental support for better school attendance?

help in assessing the operation of the 'increased parent understanding of school's expectations' mechanism.

Remember also that mechanisms may operate for some teachers, parents or children but not others. Or that they will work effectively for some, ineffectively for others. Perhaps the 'parent understanding' mechanism is operated by parental visits to homes of particular socioeconomic or ethnic background. Or it may not be effective in producing change with others because the parents already understand the school's expectations. Also mechanisms may work in some contexts or settings, not in others. And there may be mechanisms which actively inhibit desired outcomes.

The following chapter aims to assist you in working out a design which will provide answers to your evaluation questions. Or, to be more accurate, one which would in principle provide those answers. In the real world, there is no guarantee that even the best planned design will actually deliver what you need. However, with a well thought-through design and careful attention to the practicalities of running the study, you will maximize your chances of success.

Chapter 4: tasks

1. Discuss with personnel responsible for planning the program their rationale for how it is supposed to work:
    *   Talk in terms of mechanisms, contexts, etc., only if you find this congenial, and feel it will be similarly congenial to them. Otherwise refer to ideas, hypotheses, etc.
    *   Seek to establish a small set of possible mechanisms through which they consider the program to operate (and any mechanisms likely to stop it operating effectively).
    *   If you have views about its likely basis of operation (based on involvement with this program, evaluation of other programs or from more general theoretical perspectives) bring these into the discussion.

2. (*For programs already running*)   Repeat 1 above with *program personnel and others (including clients if feasible) familiar with the operation of the program.*

3. Develop a set of possible mechanisms based on 1 and 2.

4. Produce a set of evaluation questions appropriate to these mechanisms and to the other purposes of your evaluation (refer back to the task in Chapter 1).

5. For the outcome aspects of your evaluation (if any) consider: if an experimental design is indicated and feasible. Give your reasons: if not, should a quasi-experimental design be used? Give your reasons: if neither, what non-experimental design is possible?

5
GETTING ANSWERS TO EVALUATION QUESTIONS

Most of the attempts to display designs in methodologically orientated texts show sets of boxes with links and arrows between them. In my experience they are at best logical sanitized versions of design reality, bearing little resemblance to the complex, messy and interactive nature of what actually goes on. Martin's (1981) 'garbage can' model of research seems closer to it. Theories, methods, resources and solutions swirl around in the wastebasket which constitutes the decision space of the project. They are all interdependent and the design emerges from their interaction. Grady and Wallston (1988) throw in to the pot problems, phenomena and the personal concerns of the researcher for their mark-two version of the garbage can model.

However, such models provide little or no explicit guidance with the design process. So Figure 5.1 reluctantly reverts to a simple box and links approach, using terms appropriate to the task of designing a small-scale evaluation. The messages this figure seeks to communicate are as follows:

- Your *EVALUATION QUESTIONS* are central to the design process. In many evaluations, you put in a lot of work on these questions up-front before actually carrying out the evaluation. For others the appropriate questions to ask emerge during the evaluation, and perhaps some questions have to be discarded because you can't get answers to them. In any case, by the end of the process, what you have learned from the evaluation can be systematized as the answers to a set of questions.
- The *PURPOSES* of the evaluation to a large extent determine the evaluation questions.
- *THEORY* can mean many things, but one aspect which also helps in focusing the evaluation questions is the ideas behind the program, the formal or informal hypotheses or hunches of program staff and program developers about the program and how it is supposed to 'work'.
- The evaluation questions largely determine the *METHODS* (self-completion questionnaires, unstructured interviews or whatever) of data

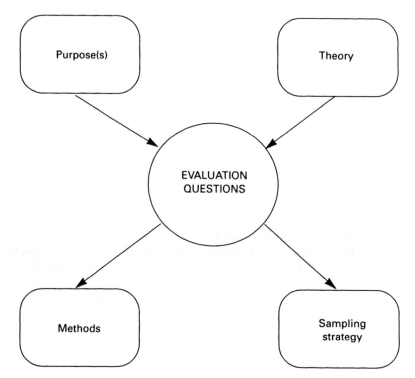

Figure 5.1 *Framework for evaluation design*

collection to be used in carrying out the evaluation. While there are no universal rules, some methods are more suitable than others for particular types of question.

- Consideration of how you will need to proceed to get answers to the questions dictates your *SAMPLING STRATEGY*. This refers to the fact that, even in a very small-scale evaluation, it is impossible to collect information and data about everyone concerned at all times and in all possible situations. Principled and thought-through selectivity is essential.

We have already considered how the purposes of the evaluation, together with a theory of how the program works, help in determining the evaluation questions. This chapter focuses on the development of an evaluation plan through making decisions about *methods* and *sampling strategy*. In other words sorting out the tactics of how you are going to collect information, who from, where, when, etc.

Methods of Collecting Information

Armed with your set of evaluation questions, you now need to consider how you can best get trustworthy answers to them. To do this, you are going to have to collect evidence, data or information in one or more forms.

Some of what you need may already be available. Management information systems or systematic monitoring procedures may have generated data it would be pointless for you to seek to duplicate. It is, however, highly likely you will have to collect data especially for the evaluation.

As indicated in Figure 5.1, the purpose and nature of the evaluation and, in particular, the questions to which you seek answers largely govern the choice of methods for gathering data. Practicalities such as the resources and time available for the work are also central. Some evaluators may start from a theoretical stance which puts a particular method in a privileged position, or rules it out of consideration. Thus, for example, a method resulting in quantitative data might be deemed essential (or anathema!). I have tried to dissuade you from such principled rigidity. A potentially tricky situation is where the sponsor of the evaluation, or other persons having a stake in the evaluation, holds strong views about the choice of methods. If their specification was for you to 'carry out a survey on . . .' then your initial task is to probe a little deeper and to seek to establish what the sponsor or organization hopes to get out of the evaluation. And to see whether or not a survey would do that job. Any mismatch between the two should be pointed out, and resolved, at the design stage.

It is worth taking serious note of the type of evidence which communicates best to the sponsor or other important audiences. Some may only be persuaded by quantitative data in the form of means and statistical analysis. Others by vivid accounts and telling quotations. Accepting this as an influence is legitimate when your task includes facilitating implementation of the findings of the evaluation.

Data Quality

Whatever means are employed to gather evidence, it is essential you worry about the quality of the data you are getting. Bored respondents in a survey may tick boxes at random or make pretty patterns. Alienated interviewees may deliberately mislead, or tell you what they think you want to hear. Experienced users of formal social science research methods are sensitized to such difficulties and there are partial solutions which are covered below in relation to specific data-collection methods. However, any single method has strengths and weaknesses in this and other respects. The fact that different methods tend to have rather different strengths and weaknesses makes a strong case for *MULTI-METHOD EVALUATIONS* – i.e. where two or more different data-collection methods are used when seeking answers to an evaluation question.

Commonsense Methods

If you are someone without previous evaluation experience or background in social science research who has been given responsibility for running an evaluation, do not despair. By working through the earlier chapters, you should now have some appreciation of the task ahead of you. You will have a feeling for the focus of the evaluation and for ethical and political considerations which need consideration. The next chapter will help to sensitise you to some of the practical issues.

Sitting at your desk and 'doing' the evaluation out of your own head without benefit of other evidence or data is definitely not recommended. Admittedly, you wouldn't be the first to do it that way, particularly if working to a very tight timescale. And, if you are an insider to the organization where the evaluation is being done, your own knowledge and experience are something which could, and should, make a significant contribution to the evaluation. However, it is inevitable you will only have a partial view, and will also have prejudices which will bias that view. So, something additional is called for, to improve and augment the information on which the evaluation is based. Others need to contribute in some way, including whenever possible in the collection and subsequent analysis of data. Such wider involvement, as argued for in Chapter 2, is likely to have the added benefit of facilitating the implementation of subsequent findings and recommendations.

In commonsense terms there are three main approaches to gathering information:

- *Observing* what is happening.
- *Talking* to those involved or otherwise getting their views or opinions.
- *Getting hold of documents*, such as minutes of meetings, program descriptions, etc.

If you use these approaches systematically, with the intention of finding answers to your evaluation questions rather than trying to 'prove' what you thought you knew already, this can go a considerable way towards a useful evaluation.

These commonsense approaches have their counterparts in the formal research methods discussed below. If you have no background in the use of these methods, you are recommended to read these sections carefully, getting a feel for the issues involved in their use. This will help you to appreciate both what you might do yourself, and what you might get others to carry out on your behalf.

Some Commonly Used Research Methods

The advantage of using formal research methods is that considerable efforts have been put in over the years to establish how they can be used to best effect. The corresponding disadvantage is that the knowledge and skill needed to use these methods successfully take time and effort to acquire. The following sections cover some key aspects of a range of possible formal methods. Further details are provided in Robson (1993) and in a range of other social sciences research methods texts including Bickman and Rog (1998).

Methods range from those which are highly prestructured (such as surveys using self-completion questionnaires) to those with little or no prestructure (such as depth interviews). While it might appear the latter constitute a kind of 'soft option' usable by those without experience, beware. It is a reasonably general rule that the less structure in the method, the more experience is needed to use it successfully. It is feasible to read up on the more structured methods and do a pretty professional job with them even without previous background. Acquiring expertise with the less structured methods takes time.

Questionnaires

Questionnaires are very widely used in small-scale evaluations. Indeed in some circles (for example, student evaluation of courses in higher education) there is an unexamined assumption that evaluation equates to asking people to fill in a questionnaire. There are reasons for this beyond simple inertia. It appears deceptively straightforward to devise the questions. Completion of the questionnaire doesn't take long, and can be incorporated without undue difficulty into the process. With forethought, the task of analysis can be routinised, and it can generate satisfying quantitative data.

There are some underlying problems, however. Good questionnaires are not easy to devise, as is testified by the prevalence of many awful examples. More fundamentally, the choice of a questionnaire should be governed by the evaluation questions. So if, for example, the main purpose of an evaluation is to assess whether the program goals have been achieved, then you only use a questionnaire if it will help to do that.

Surveys and questionnaires. Surveys typically involve the collection of a relatively small amount of information in standardized form from a relatively large number of people, usually, but not necessarily, by means of a questionnaire. They are very widely used in social research and in applied fields such as market research and political polling. However, formal surveys have a limited role within most small-scale evaluations. Their main application is within needs analyses, as discussed in Appendix A.

Much of the effort in using surveys is up-front – in the design phase. It is straightforward to put together a set of questions for a survey questionnaire, but it is surprisingly difficult to generate a well crafted set which are understandable and unambiguous, and relevant to the evaluation questions. The savings in effort with surveys arise when this well designed instrument can then be used with a large group of people, particularly when they complete it themselves. Small-scale evaluations are likely to involve small numbers of people, although needs analyses are not necessarily restricted in this respect.

Surveys are particularly useful when the intention is to collect simple descriptive information about the numbers and proportions of people who possess a particular attribute such as being male or female, falling within a certain age range or coming from a particular ethnic background. (Note that even here considerable care will have to be given to the exact phrasing of questions on age and ethnicity.) Mail or postal surveys appear an attractive option in some situations but may suffer from low response rates. Mangione (1998) provides a practical discussion of the steps needed to produce a high-quality mail survey.

Response rates and sampling. If everyone involved is asked to complete the questionnaire, then the main concern is to try to set things up so that virtually everyone does actually complete it. Logically, you do not know how anyone who does not complete the questionnaire would have responded. If there are significant numbers of non-responders, this can seriously reduce its usefulness and credibility. It is rarely possible to make a plausible claim that this does not introduce a bias. For example, it might be that mothers from a particular ethnic background are both less likely to complete a questionnaire about maternity services, and also to have more concerns about it. Poor response rates to the questionnaire would lead to a positive bias in overall ratings about the service. Although it is of course possible to separate out responses from different ethnic groups if this information has been collected, you still have no guarantee those not responding from a particular ethnic group would have given similar patterns of response to those for whom you have the information.

A needs analysis might work on the basis of a sample survey, i.e. where responses are sought from some proportion of the overall group. In this situation there are additional worries about how representative of the whole those selected are. Unless it is possible to ensure all those within the group have the same chance of being selected (a so-called random sample), it is very difficult to defend your results from accuzations of possible bias.

These worries may be thought of as being unnecessarily pernickety in simple small-scale evaluations. In many such cases they probably are. What one does is one's best in seeking to get the highest possible response rate and guarding against likely biases. Given this, you then give an honest account of the shortcomings of the survey findings. However, simply because there is a well developed methodology of survey research, it is not difficult for someone critical of your evaluation findings to discredit them if they rely on surveys which do not meet professional standards.

Sources of questions. Start with what you are trying to achieve by asking a question (the question objective) and then try to devise the appropriate question to do this. Fowler (1998) gives a helpful and readable set of suggestions for how this might be done. The basic principles that he suggests are summarized in Figure 5.2. The question objectives themselves derive from your evaluation questions. (Note that evaluation questions and survey questions are, of course, different things; however, the suggestions made for devising understandable and unambiguous survey questions may help with writing your evaluation questions.)

1) The strength of survey research is asking people about their first-hand experiences: what they have done, their current situations, their feelings and perceptions. Yet, surprisingly, a good bit of survey research is devoted to asking people questions to which most people do not have informed answers. Beware of:

   a. asking about information that is only acquired second hand;
   b. hypothetical questions;
   c. asking about perceptions of causality; and
   d. asking about solutions to complex problems.

2) Questions should be asked one at a time:

   a. Avoid asking two questions at once.
   b. Avoid questions that impose unwarranted assumptions.
   c. Beware of questions that include hidden contingencies.

3) A survey question should be worded so that all respondents are answering the same question:

   a. To the extent possible, choose the words in questions so that all respondents understand their meaning and all respondents have the same sense of what the meaning is.
   b. To the extent that words or terms must be used that have meanings that are likely not to be shared, provide definitions to all respondents.
   c. The time period referred to by a question should be unambiguous.
   d. If what is to be covered is too complex to be included in a single question, ask multiple questions.

4) If a survey is to be interviewer administered, wording of the questions must constitute a complete and adequate script such that when the interviewer reads the question as worded, the respondent will be fully prepared to answer the question:

   a. If definitions are to be given, give them before the question itself is asked.
   b. A question should end with the question itself. If there are response alternatives, arrange the question so they constitute the final part.

5) All respondents should understand the kind of answer that constitutes an adequate answer to a question:

   a. Avoid questions that begin with adverbs: how, when, where, why, to what extent. Such questions do not specify the terms of an adequate answer.
   b. Specify the number of responses to be given to questions for which more than one answer is possible.

6) Survey instruments should be designed so the tasks of reading questions, following instructions, and recording answers are as easy as possible for interviewers and respondents.

Figure 5.2   *Principles of survey questionnaire design*
Source: Adapted from Fowler (1998, pp. 365–6).

The following sources should help provide both evaluation and survey questions:

- Stakeholders, in particular decision-makers.
- Program staff and clients (through observation and discussion prior

to the survey; this will also help to ensure questions are phrased in terms of the language they use – particularly jargon).
• Questionnaires used for similar purposes by yourself or others; this can save time and effort, and may help to make comparisons with other programs.

Figure 5.3 suggests the kind of areas that might be covered by a questionnaire in a small-scale evaluation.

A note on measures of client satisfaction. The 'satisfaction' questionnaire commonly used in hotels and in many other customer situations is so widely used it almost qualifies as a 'commonsense' method. However, while it is easy to produce such a questionnaire, it is not straightforward to produce a good one. If you are intending to do this, you are recommended to read the section on questionnaires below. Figure 5.4 provides a very simple example.

Relying on a simple client satisfaction measure of this kind represents an extreme minimalist approach to evaluation, even for a very small-scale evaluation. However, there is certainly something to be said for assessing client satisfaction as a contribution to outcome measures. If clients

---

Categories of Question
Note: The general criterion for inclusion of a question is that it will help in answering your evaluation questions.

1) Covering the backgrounds of participants:
   • General factual information on demographics such as age, socioeconomic status, family size, educational and ethnic background.
   • Specific information relevant to the particular evaluation, e.g. number of previous children for maternity unit study.
   To include only those aspects relevant to your evaluation questions. You can include requests for other information you have a hunch may be relevant, providing you are convinced it would not be sensitive or embarrassing – otherwise no 'fishing trips'.
   Use: Potentially useful in all approaches to evaluation, i.e. in evaluation of needs, processes, outcomes and efficiency.

2) Covering what they have actually done on the program:
   • Assesses implementation of the program; possible discrepancies between what was planned and delivered.
   Use: Mainly useful in evaluation of processes, but potentially useful in all approaches to evaluation.

3) Covering what they got from the program:
   • Assesses perceived changes from participants' perspectives.
   • Assesses extent to which this meets participants' needs.
   Use: Mainly useful in support of evaluation of outcomes (together with other more objective measures) and of needs evaluation, but potentially useful in all approaches to evaluation.

4) Covering ways in which the program might be improved:
   Use: For virtually all evaluations.

Figure 5.3 *Possible sections in a questionnaire for a small-scale evaluation*

EVALUATION SHEET

Your views on the following points would be appreciated.
All responses are anonymous and will simply be used to assist in the
development of the   residential weekend. Completion is voluntary but
exercises of this kind are much more valuable when everybody gives their
views.

Please circle the number of your COHORT   1   2   3

1)   Any comments on the PRESENTATION sessions?

2)   Any comments on the OTHER (Discussions; Small groups; 1:1)
     sessions?

3)   Any comments on OTHER ASPECTS of the weekend?

4)   Any suggestions for IMPROVING THE RESIDENTIAL WEEKEND?

Figure 5.4   *Example of a simple 'client satisfaction' questionnaire*

dislike a program then it is unlikely to have their active involvement, participation or support. If the questionnaire does reveal major areas of dissatisfaction, it is obviously sensible to do something about that. You only compound the problem by asking for views and then not taking note of them.

Diaries

Asking clients, and sometimes others such as program personnel, to keep a diary during their involvement with the program can be a very useful method of obtaining their views and impressions. Its central feature is that they are encouraged to write something on a regular, usually daily, basis which helps in getting feedback close in time to the actual experience. It is substantially less intrusive and low cost than interviewing or presenting them with a questionnaire each day.

The diary can take many forms, ranging from a set of quite detailed daily questionnaires bound together, to a blank page for each day. A relatively flexible format, but with some focusing prompts, is commonly used; Figure 5.5 provides an example. An added bonus of this approach, noted by participants in Johnson (1997), is that completing the diary can facilitate their reflection about the experience and help them to analyse it. This is likely to be of benefit not only to the evaluation, but also to the effectiveness of the program itself. Note that this is an example of the way in which the process of evaluation can actually modify the thing being evaluated. While this reactivity is in one sense a methodological problem, it might be argued such beneficial effects are a good thing. Perhaps the lesson to be learned is that diary completion would be a valuable addition to the program itself!

Day One

        ✔ what activities you have been involved in
        ✔ the time and place of these, in the order which they happened
        ✔ what was useful?
        ✔ what was not useful?
        ✔ what would have been useful?

(full page – same format for each day)

Reflections on the week

Please give a brief description of your overall impressions of the week.

Do you feel prepared for your course?

Any other comments?

Please keep this diary for the next week and then complete the standard questionnaire overleaf.

Figure 5.5 *Example of a diary*

Source: From Johnson (1997, pp. 356–9).

Interviewing

The interview is, deservedly, a widely used method in small-scale evaluations. It comes in many different forms. Typically, it takes place in a face-to-face situation with one interviewer and one interviewee. However, group interviews are possible, and interviews conducted over the telephone are increasingly used. The latter can produce substantial savings in time and cost, although there are disadvantages arising from the lack of direct personal contact (see Lavrakas, 1998).

Three broad styles of conducting interviews worth considering are *informal interviews, semi-structured interviews* and *structured interviews*.

Informal interviews. When you are involved with a program, perhaps observing what is happening when it is in operation, opportunities commonly arise to have brief discussions with program staff, or with managers, or clients. Such conversations can be invaluable in developing an understanding of what is going on, and these various persons' perceptions about this. At an early stage of involvement, your agenda is likely to be exploratory. As you develop and refine the evaluation questions to which you seek answers, these conversations can be more closely focused.

It may well be your interviewees do not view these informal chats as interviews and there is no need for you to label them as such. Calling them interviews may well reduce their spontaneity. Providing there is a clear understanding that you are present in the situation in the role of evaluator, the omission does not appear unethical.

The value of these sessions depends crucially on your conversational skills. You are called upon to relate to people in a range of different positions. You will need to think on your feet when generating questions to understand and develop the points made to you, without doing this in a way which imposes your own perceptions and categories upon others.

It is important you capture any insights gained from these informal talks. Whenever feasible, seize the opportunity of making notes about what was said, if possible with word-for-word quotations, shortly after the discussion. They often occur at coffee or lunchbreaks and there can be time to do this before moving on to some other activity. If the discussion takes place during a continuing session, then notes can be made under the guise of recording observation.

Depth interviews. Unless you have had prior training, it is probably wisest to restrict your use of unstructured interviews to these short informal sessions. In unstructured interviews, sometimes called depth interviews, the task of the interviewer is to facilitate and encourage the interviewee to reveal in depth any aspects they wish to bring up. This is a task calling for considerable sensitivity and experience and should not be approached lightly without this background. It is all too easy to stray from the task of gathering information relevant to the evaluation, to some inappropriate amateur counselling on personal or professional problems.

Semi-structured interviews. A semi-structured interview is one where the interviewer has worked out in advance the main areas he wishes to cover, but is free to vary the exact wording of questions as well as their ordering. So, if an interviewee starts to cover a new area in response to a question, then the interviewer keeps the flow going by asking relevant questions on his list of topics. Any missing topics are returned to by the end of the interview.

The set of topics is sometimes referred to as an interview guide. Careful thought and preparation are needed to help ensure you maximize the chance of gathering information relevant to your evaluation questions. In this way you can most profitably use the limited time available for interviews. It is good practice to have the guide accessible when you are conducting the interviews, hence giving you an aide-mémoire to check all topics have been covered. In some situations where rapport with the interviewees is important and possibly problematic, it helps to have memorized the topics so you do not break the flow. Figure 5.6 Provides an example of an interview guide. The specificity of guides will vary considerably from one study to another, depending on the extent to which it is feasible to prespecify the topics. Interviews at an early stage of an evaluation, or where the program itself is at an early developmental stage, would be less detailed.

In practice, many interviews in small-scale evaluations are likely to be semi-structured. They can be particularly useful when the interview takes place in a group setting. They do require some preparation but this is not exorbitant. The flexibility in delivery of the interview sits well with the usual requirements of having a relatively small number of interviews with different categories of interviewees (such as program administrators and clients), for which different phrasing and other use of language may be necessary to communicate effectively.

Structured interviews. A fully structured interview where there is a fixed sequence of predetermined questions is essentially the same thing as a self-completion questionnaire. It has the advantage of being in a social situation where someone who is good at interviewing can build up empathy between herself and the interviewee, leading it is hoped to a greater involvement and better quality data. Even if this does not occur, the interviewer is in the position of being able to assess the degree of the interviewee's interest and involvement. There are, as ever, corresponding disadvantages. Interviewees may feel the need to appear in a good light and, obviously, it calls for the interviewer's time.

It can be used exclusively with closed (yes/no; or choice from a fixed set of alternative answers) questions and in appearance is essentially the same as a self-completion questionnaire. However, some open-ended questions can be included; the instructions to the interviewer might then include indications of any 'probes' to elicit further information, as shown in Figure 5.6.

This type of standardized interview is used when it is important to

Note: An initial interview prior to client's involvement with the program. The main interest here is on what clients bring to the program. This is to be linked to later interviews.

Topics to be covered

1) Introduction by interviewer:
   - who you are and what you are doing;
   - request to tape interview – if unwilling, request to take notes;
   - assurance on confidentiality and anonymity;
   - purpose and length of interview; and
   - reason for choice of interviewee.
2) Prior knowledge about program.
3) Reasons for joining the program.
4) Previous involvement with this type of program.
   - feelings/views about this.
5) Expectations/anticipations about joining this program:
   - worries/fears?
   - likely difficulties?
   - what are you looking forward to?
6) Family responsibilities/commitments?
   - management while involved with the program; and
   - attitude of husband/wife/partner to your involvement.
7) Other interests/activities which might affect (or be affected by) your involvement with the program?
8) Other things which might cause difficulties?
   - money
   - travel arrangements.
9) Any other issues about the program and your involvement with it?
10) Biographical details.
11) Willingness to be interviewed later?
12) Thanks.

Figure 5.6   Example of an interview guide

Source: Adapted and abridged from Johnson (1997, pp. 347–8).

minimize variability from one interviewee to another. The data obtained are then more easily compared with less risk of bias occurring simply because different people are being asked rather different questions. Even so the analysis and interpretation of open-ended responses are not straightforward (see Chapter 6).

One situation where this type of interview might be preferred is where there are several persons carrying out the interviewing. This can occur in some small-scale evaluations with a participatory approach. For example, some program staff or other key stakeholders might act as interviewers. It appears likely that, left to their own devices, they would ask questions in different ways, particularly if they do not have previous interviewing experience. With a detailed structured interview schedule, and clear instructions that it should be followed closely, the effects of having different interviewers can be minimised.

Question wording in structured interviews. The specific wording of questions can be very important. If an interviewee does not understand a question, or if different interviewees understand it differently, there is little chance of getting worthwhile data. The wording of closed questions was discussed earlier in connection with self-completion questionnaires (see page 83) and the same points can be made about the wording of such questions in interview settings.

Figure 5.7 covers some of the main issues involved in the wording of open-ended questions.

Combining Interview Styles

The styles discussed in the previous sections can be combined in various ways to suit the particular circumstances of an evaluation. It may be sensible to have an interview guide worked out with a set of topic areas you seek to explore opportunistically in informal interviews. Often there is merit in having combined semi-structured and fully structured sessions. Perhaps there is a small set of specific questions you wish to ask everyone, and a number of topic areas which can be explored in a more flexible way.

The wording of any open-ended questions is particularly important in structured interviews where exactly the same wording should be used in different interviews. However, the same principles of question wording apply in other types of interview whenever the intention is to present an open-ended question.

The wording of the question should:

- Allow the interviewee to respond in their own terms. It should not seek to pre-specify the dimension on which response is to be made. For example:

  What is your opinion about the first phase of the program? is open-ended in this sense, whereas

  How satisfied are you by the first phase of the program? prespecifies the dimension of satisfaction (if this is the dimension of interest to you, then it would probably be better to provide a list of response possibilities, or a scale that could be quantified).

- Be clearly understandable to interviewees. It helps considerably to know the terms they use to describe the program and any other things you want to know about (it may be necessary to use more than one term if different categories of persons are to be interviewed – for example, prisoners and prison warders will have different words to describe aspects of prison life).

- Be sensitive to the possible effects of questions. It is clearly impossible to predict all possible reactions to a question. However, forethought and knowledge, both of the situation and of those you are interviewing, can help you to avoid many pitfalls. Patton (1982, p. 172) suggests ways of providing contexts to questions which can reduce the personal and intrusive impact of potentially sensitive questioning, e.g. the use of 'simulation' questions such as 'suppose I was present with you during a group therapy session, what would I see happening?'

Figure 5.7 *The wording of open-ended questions*

During the course of an evaluation, it is not uncommon to move from informal to more formal interviewing. Initially the task is primarily to explore and get a feeling for what is going on. Subsequently, when there is greater clarity, one may be looking for more systematic information from a group of clients who have completed the program when evaluating outcomes.

Social desirability effects. People are likely to respond in a way that puts them in a good light. This is more likely to happen when the questions are asked by an interviewer than when they complete the questionnaire for themselves. It is also helpful to stress the confidentiality of answers. As it is often difficult to guess which questions may embarrass, it is good practice to try to phrase all questions so the possibility of revealing negative aspects of oneself in any answer is minimised.

Focus Groups

A focus group is effectively a type of semi-structured interview carried out in a group setting. It has been much used in market research, including recently that carried out by political parties in developing policies. It is a widely used method in needs analysis but can be used for several evaluative purposes. Figure 5.8 suggests some of the common uses.

In the jargon the person running the group is known as a 'facilitator', whose role is to 'guide' the discussion. A list of about half a dozen topic areas is selected, and turned into question form. The convention is to have between eight and a dozen group members. Sessions typically run from one and a half to two hours. However, none of these aspects is sacrosanct; nor is the market research tradition of providing liberal supplies of food and drink!

The main benefit of group interviews is the possibility of additional insights being gained through the interaction of ideas and suggestions from group members. In practice, the quality of information from a focus group depends crucially on the skills of the facilitator. They need to

---

1) Obtaining general background information about a topic of interest.
2) Generating research hypotheses that can be submitted to further research and testing using more quantitative approaches.
3) Stimulating new ideas and creative concepts.
4) Diagnosing the potential for problems with a new program, service or product.
5) Generating impressions of products, programs, services, institutions or other objects of interest.
6) Learning how respondents talk about the phenomenon of interest (which may, in turn, facilitate the design of questionnaires, survey instruments or other research tools that might be employed in more quantitative research).
7) Interpreting previously obtained quantitative results.

Figure 5.8 *Common uses of focus groups*

Source: From Stewart and Shamdasani (1998, pp. 506–7).

exercise a light control so that, without this appearing artificial, all members are encouraged to contribute. The danger is that one or two people, and their views, dominate the discussion such that more reserved members do not feel able to speak.

Their main advantage is in collecting data from a group of people much more quickly and cheaply than with separate interviews. Also they can be set up easily in situations where a survey might not be practicable. Their disadvantages are partly linked to the very common use of convenience sampling – i.e. groups tend to be made up of those people easily available, and prepared to give up two or more hours of their time. This is not a necessary feature, however, and carefully selected samples could be used. Even in that situation there is probably limited generalizability of findings as they will depend on the complex interactions between group members and the facilitator and even apparently closely similar groups can generate very different answers to the questions posed. Stewart and Shamdasani (1998) provide a balanced and detailed account of the uses of focus groups.

Recording Interview Data

The data from interviews consist of what people say. You are after actual quotations, word for word. There may be some closed-question answers collected at interview simply because this was more convenient than having them fill in a questionnaire. These can be dealt with as if a questionnaire had been used.

There is much to be said for tape-recording all interviews other than short informal ones. For the latter, tape-recording would destroy the informality and every effort should be made to capture any noteworthy quotations as soon as feasible after the discussion, as discussed above on page 89.

By tape-recording formal interviews you can concentrate on the task of carrying out a quality interview where you develop a good rapport with your interviewee and keep it going along at a good, natural pace. There may be some situations where it is not possible to record; perhaps because permission is refused either by the interviewee or some gatekeeper. Or because the topic is highly sensitive and you feel, or are advised, that recording would be intrusive. Or even because your recorder won't work properly. Figure 5.9 covers some simple practical points about the use of tape-recorders. Apologies for including the blindingly obvious, but experience suggest that interviewers and tape-recorders often do not go well together.

In situations where recording is not possible, you should make as full notes as possible at the time. Try to develop a system of abbreviations and to get word-for-word quotations. Don't be afraid of stopping the interview to make sure you have captured important quotations. Although this obviously breaks the flow, interviewees will usually accept this if you make clear you are doing this because you thought they said

Before using a tape-recorder to record an interview make sure that
(before the session):

- You know how it works! Practise using it so you are familiar with all the con-
  trols and in particular know how to record and play-back. If there is a separate
  microphone make sure you know how to use it including turning it on and off.
- There are new batteries and you have at least one spare set. Check you know
  how to replace batteries.
- You have a new tape. Preferably a C90 giving 45 minutes play on each side.
  Have similar spare tapes to at least twice the expected duration of the planned
  interview session.
- You get satisfactory recorded sound quality, preferably under the exact conditions under which the recordings will take place. If necessary seek technical
  advice as to how quality might be improved (e.g. by use of more sensitive microphone, lapel mikes, etc.). Note it is notoriously difficult to get good sound quality
  from group interviews – seek advice.

(at the session)

- You have permission from the interviewee and any relevant others to tape.
- The recorder works satisfactorily with acceptable sound quality.
- You rewind the tape, and set to record.
- You are alert for the end of the tape and turn it over. Go on to further tapes if
  necessary.

(after the session)

- Check quality of recorded sound. If it is not satisfactory take steps to improve it
  before the next interview session.

Figure 5.9 *Practicalities of tape-recording*

something important. If possible, fill these notes out immediately after
the interview making sure everything is legible and understandable. If
this is not feasible, it must be done the same day. If you leave it any
longer, you are in great danger of not being able to understand them
when you come to analyse what you have got from the interview.

It is good practice to make some notes even when the interview is
taped. They are particularly helpful when you are not able to do a full
transcript (see below), provide something of an insurance against possible taping problems and can remind you of non-verbal features. You can
also note ideas or thoughts that come to you which may help in subsequent interpretation; differentiate these in some way, perhaps by putting
them in brackets.

Transcribing interviews. Getting a full transcript of an audio-tape of an
interview is very time-consuming. A half-hour tape can easily take
several hours to transcribe, particularly if you are new to the task. You
need to budget for this, either in terms of your own time, or in terms of
the money for the services of an audio-typist.

While a full transcript is desirable, as it provides the easiest basis for
subsequent analysis, it is not essential. By listening to the tape several

times, you will be able to highlight the important quotations. Your interview notes, made at the time, can be supplemented by reference to tape counter numbers corresponding to these quotations or by transcripts of the quotations themselves.

Observation

The main contribution that observation can make to a small-scale evaluation is to help understand the program and how it is working. To do this calls for a fluid, exploratory and relatively unstructured approach to observation which leads to qualitative data. It is possible to observe using highly structured approaches to observation, which are covered briefly below. However, these call for very specialized techniques and have limited usefulness in small-scale evaluations.

Spending time with a program and getting a feel for what is happening simply by keeping your eyes and ears open can be extremely valuable. This is particularly so in evaluations of process but it can inform all kinds of evaluations. It combines naturally with the use of informal interviews, where having observed something, you take up any opportunity that then arises to discuss it with one or more of those involved.

This type of observation is similar to the participant observation carried out by social anthropologists and some sociologists when they take an ethnographic approach. 'Ethnography is the art and science of describing a group or culture. The description may be of a small tribal group in some exotic land or of a classroom in middle-class suburbia' (Fetterman, 1998, p. 473). It typically involves an immersion in that culture which, classically, would take anything from several months to two or three years. In small-scale evaluations this kind of time-scale is out of the question. However, while it is not feasible to carry out an ethnography as such, ethnographic methods can be used. Fetterman (1989; 1998) provides detailed, very readable accounts.

Participant observation may be carried out covertly or overtly. Covertly means that those being observed do not know of your evaluative role. There are few situations where this is ethically justifiable and hence it is assumed here that normally you will only observe in situations where this role has been made explicit. There are also different degrees of participation. Adler and Adler (1987) differentiate between:

- *peripheral member*, where you observe and interact closely enough with members to establish an insider's perspective but do not take part in their activities;
- *active member*, where you are more involved in group activities without a full commitment to the program; and
- *complete member*, where you are evaluating a program with which you are already fully involved (e.g. as program staff or as a client) or where you seek to be so involved.

Some evaluators (e.g. Posovac and Carey, 1997, p. 218) regard what are here referred to as peripheral member roles as being non-participant observation. The exact definition is not central, provided both yourself and those taking part in the program understand and accept your role. My preference would be to restrict the notion of non-participant observation to those rare situations where the evaluation is taking place in some public setting and the evaluator has no direct interaction with those involved. An example might be in the evaluation of the behaviour of the public at an exhibition where observation takes place behind a one-way screen and the identity of individuals is not known. Incidentally, this is one situation where covert observation appears justifiable.

Generally the greater the participation the more you are likely to have an effect on the working of the program, but the easier it becomes to understand what is happening from the point of view of those involved. It is a difficult balance to strike, although in practice you may not have much choice about the degree of participation. One stance is to get as close as you can to fulfilling an insider role but 'hanging back'. In other words being the kind of insider who is pretty unobtrusive.

The task of observing what is happening might at first sight appear deceptively simple. However, and somewhat paradoxically, particularly in very familiar situations, it may seem very little is happening. Or, conversely, so much is happening one doesn't know where to focus. Patterns and regularities are likely to become apparent with prolonged exposure to the situation, but it may be helpful to have some categorization of the things you might attend to. Figure 5.10 gives one way of doing this. Note the inclusion of 'unobtrusive measures'. These are sometimes referred to as the 'traces' produced by a program and can often add an additional dimension to your data gathering. They can be very varied depending on the nature of the program. For example, in a school setting they might include presence or absence of litter or graffiti either in the classroom or elsewhere, material on blackboards or noticeboards, etc. Generally any individual trace is not easily interpretable by itself. It is only when some pattern appears to emerge, or they support understandings obtained from interviews or other sources of data. This potentially collaborative feature of data obtained by means of different methods is known as *triangulation* (Denzin, 1988), by analogy with the process in surveying where better understanding is achieved by taking a view of something from different perspectives. It is an important way of improving the credibility of findings, particularly when they are based on qualitative data.

Observation of this type of information is in some ways similar to the use of existing records and documents as discussed below (see also Webb *et al.*, 1981).

Structured observation. A very different style of observation involves the use of structured observation schedules. This calls for the setting up of a number of predefined observational categories, perhaps concerning the behaviour of clients or some other activities. The task is then to note the occurrence of these categories. Sometimes the sequence of different

---

1) *Program setting.* The physical environment within which the program takes place should be described in sufficient detail to permit the reader to visualize the setting.

2) *Human and social environment.* Look for ways in which people organize themselves into groups and subgroups.

3) *Program activities and participant behaviours:*
   - What do people do in the program?
   - How do they experience the program?
   - What is it like to be a participant in the program?
   - What would one see if one were watching the program in progress?
   - For planned units of activity (e.g. a program session), what happens at the beginning; during the activity; and at the end?

4) *Informal interactions and unplanned activities.* Collect information about what people do and what they are saying to each other.

5) *The 'native' language of the program participants.* Note the terms they use to describe the program, the people involved, and what is happening (useful for interviews).

6) *Non-verbal communication* (e.g. means of attracting attention, physical spacing and arrangements).

7) *Unobtrusive measures.* These include physical clues about program activities (e.g., dusty equipment, areas used a lot or a little).

8) *Observing what does not happen.* If the program goals, implementation design or proposal suggest certain things ought to happen or are expected to happen, note if those things did not happen.

Figure 5.10 *Suggestions for foci of observation*

Source: Adapted from Patton (1990). Mertens (1998, pp. 319–20) uses a similar but more detailed schema.

behaviours or activities is noted, or the number of times a particular activity takes place within a given period.

The construction of a worthwhile observation schedule of this kind is not an easy task. It requires considerable technical expertise and many hours of piloting to establish it has acceptable *reliability* (consistency between different observers and at different times) and *validity* (that it measures what you want it to measure). An alternative possibility is to use an already existing, pretested schedule. There are large numbers in existence. However, a version of the well-known Murphy's law (if anything can go wrong, it will) makes it highly likely any already existing schedule will not cover the particular behaviours or activities that interest you. Unfortunately, any modification of such a schedule calls for further testing and piloting to re-establish its reliability and validity. Robson (1993, pp. 206–26) provides an introductory account and further references.

There are some fields, particularly health related, where structured observational schedules are widely used and where it is more likely you will be able to pick something appropriate 'off the shelf'. Structured observation can obviously be used in situations where program outcomes are expressed in terms of an existing schedule (for example, the improvement of 'quality of life' as measured by a particular schedule), or where such a schedule provides an acceptable way of assessing these outcomes.

Using Tests and Scales

A structured observation schedule is one form of standardized measurement instrument. A wide variety of standardized tests and scales have been devised for use in different fields, some involving observation, while others require interaction with the client, or are based on self-completion.

In education, for example, there is common use of written achievement tests. Hence many evaluations of educational programs rely to some extent on such tests, possibly using a multiple-choice format. Given their high reliability and acceptability in educational settings, they are frequently used to measure both outcomes and needs. Anastasi (1988), Kline (1986; 1993) and Loewenthal (1996) give examples.

In health settings, particularly relating to mental health, standard tests can be readily found to assess many of the states such as stress, anxiety and depression, likely to be targeted by therapeutic interventions. Cheetham et al. (1992, Chap. 7) give detailed examples of the use of such scales in areas of social welfare bordering on the health sphere. Figure 5.11 suggests some general criteria for the selection of schedules.

Look for a schedule (test, checklist) which:

- *Provides answers to questions you seek answers to.* This may be in connection with outcomes, needs, processes or any other aspect, but unless this criterion is satisfied don't use the test.
- *Has acceptably high reliability.* Note there are many different ways of assessing reliability; for many of these you should be looking for a coefficient of at least 0.7. See Loewenthal (1996, pp. 9–12).
- *Provides some evidence about its validity.* Validity is assessed in several different ways. See Loewenthal (1996, pp. 12–14). Be suspicious of any schedule which does not give information about its validity.
- *Appears appropriate to your target group.* Ideally it should have been developed with essentially the same group, but this is unlikely and you have to make a qualitative judgement about appropriateness.
- *Uses language readily understandable by your target group.* Changing the language changes the schedule. However, it is better to modify the language to make it understandable (which may affect reliability, validity and comparability to results others obtain) than present something which is incomprehensible.
- *Makes acceptable demands on your target group.* In terms of time, sensitivity of items, etc.
- *You can administer.* Avoid tests calling for specialist training, unless you can get a trained person to do it for you.

Figure 5.11 *Criteria for selection of a schedule*

Documents, Records and Other Existing Information

There are likely to be already in existence several sources of information relevant to your evaluation. Many public organizations are voracious users of paper, producing documents on the planning and development of programs, including proposals, memoranda, minutes of meetings, etc. You should know what is in existence, and try to negotiate access to anything which appears relevant.

Various records will be kept of employees in businesses and other organizations. Education establishments, social services departments, criminal justice agencies and health-service providers will typically have very detailed information about their clients and their personnel. Programs are often planned to have outcomes such that their success or otherwise can be assessed with reference to existing records. For example, a program to deal with the problem of truancy in schools will be likely to include outcome data on school attendance patterns. This will be obtainable from school registers and returns made to local education authorities.

Problems in the use of pre-existing data. By definition, pre-existing data will have been originally collected for purposes other than your evaluation. This allows for the operation of a version of Murphy's law once again. Here, if data are collected for one purpose, they are likely to be in a form which makes them unusable for another purpose. If you are in on the design stage of a program it may be feasible to incorporate changes in routine data collection which will make it easier to use the data for a subsequent evaluation of the program. Or it might be possible to change slightly either the proposed program or its evaluation so that relevant questions can be answered with existing data.

Many existing records provide data about individuals, while evaluations may call for group or average data. This is not in itself a problem, and the derivation of such data may well be of more general interest than simply for the purposes of your evaluation.

There may be problems concerning the freedom of the individual and safeguards such as Data Protection Acts. This is mainly in connection with the use of records, if you are seeking to use data for a purpose other than those for which it was first collected. In line with the general need for evaluations to be carried out with strict concern for ethical considerations, you should establish whether there are any problems in your situation.

The quality of pre-existing data can be a serious problem. Even apparently factual records can be open to question, particularly when they reflect in some way on the performance of an organization. Schools which are under scrutiny for low attendance or pupil performance records, or police forces expected to show improving crime clear-up figures, may find ways of massaging such figures to their advantage. There are no easy solutions to such problems. A good inside knowledge of what actually happens is probably the best safeguard.

Similar problems occur with documents originally prepared for purposes other than the evaluation. The hope and expectation is you and others involved in evaluating a program are motivated to establish the 'truth' in the sense of seeking to provide an unbiased account. You should always consider the purposes of reports and other documents. It may well be, quite legitimately, that they are seeking to make out a case for a particular course of action.

The main safeguard is not to use pre-existing data as the sole or primary source of information about an evaluation question, unless you can satisfy yourself and others there are no obvious sources of bias, or when the likely bias is in an opposite direction from the effect found. Existing documentary evidence is best used to supplement, and give illustrative examples of, findings obtained from data you have gathered for yourself. See Hodder (1994) for a comprehensive discussion on the use of documents and records.

Sampling

The previous section on methods of collecting information covers the set of tools you might use to get answers to the evaluation questions. However, you not only need the tools, you need to decide who you are going to interview, where and when you are going to observe, which records you are going to select, and so on. In other words you need a sampling strategy. Figure 5.12 makes some suggestions about how you might go about this. The exercise of thinking through what needs to be

---

Decisions have to be made about:

- *Who* you gather information from. This includes the kinds or categories of people, as well as the specific persons within a category.
- *Where* the data collection is done.
- *When* you do it. Always at the same time or systematically or randomly different.
- *What* is sampled. You may be interested in particular events, or activities, or processes.

The intention is to gather information relevant to your evaluation questions. A principle of sampling who, where, when and what should be to try to get unbiased answers. You don't simply go for those known, or likely, to have particular views – nor do you exclude them. Random sampling will rarely be possible (though it shouldn't be ruled out).

From a practical point of view, efficiency is very important, i.e. getting the maximum amount of unbiased information for minimum use of resources. Avoid approaches to sampling which give low yields of data.

Sampling is usually relatively straightforward and obvious in outcome evaluations. It needs considerable forethought in process evaluations as there are typically many more possibilities.

Figure 5.12 *Sampling in small-scale evaluations*

sampled to gain good information about a set of evaluation questions can be salutary. An assessment of the necessary time and effort, compared with the resources you have available and the timescale within which results are expected, commonly shows you are proposing to bite off more than you can possibly chew. Chapter 6 gives some guidelines for estimating time and resource needs you might find useful in coming to realistic sampling decisions.

Even with a small program there is no way you, or others involved with the evaluation, can be everywhere it is going on, at all times and places with all the people involved. It is a physical impossibility and even if you could approximate this, it would generate a frightening amount of potential information and lead to cognitive overload (i.e. can't take it all in) on your part.

It may be worth emphasizing this use of sampling is wider than *statistical sampling*. In the latter, the idea is that by use of some procedure such as random sampling from a known population, it becomes possible to make statistical generalizations from what is found out about the sample to the likely state of affairs within the population as a whole. Here, you are certainly interested in dealing with samples which are representative rather than biased. For example, you wouldn't usually restrict your interviews to staff known to be disaffected and cynical – unless this is in itself relevant to a particular evaluation question. However, it is unlikely to be feasible to sample people on a random basis in a small-scale evaluation and you will be seeking representativeness through more intuitive approaches.

This view of sampling chimes in closely with the realist approach discussed in the previous chapter. The realist concern for establishing what works best for whom and in what context drove the search for possible mechanisms. So in sampling people, we are selecting those indicated by a mechanism; and in sampling settings, we are looking for contexts in which that mechanism operates for that subgroup of people.

Prespecified v. Emergent Designs

The extent to which you can, or should, specify in detail exactly what you are going to do, and how you are going to do it, before starting on the data-gathering phase of an evaluation, will vary considerably from one study to another. As with other aspects, you may be locked into a very tight specification by the sponsor and other key stakeholders, and the agreement you make with them. Or they may wish to leave it to you to get on with it.

Generally, questions to do with outcomes call for a considerable degree of prespecification, particularly where the main thrust is towards an assessment of whether known goals or objectives have been achieved. This is likely to include detailed consideration of the measures to be used and how they are to be operationalized, together with a similarly detailed sampling strategy. If an experimental or quasi-experimental design is selected, this will demand substantial preplanning on design matters including exact specification of the means of allocation to experimental and control or comparison groups.

Unless you can call on previous experience in the specific field of the program to be evaluated (your own experience or that of others you can get hold of) sensible and rational prespecification of many of these features is very difficult. One way forward in the absence of such experience is to split the evaluation into two phases. The first is primarily exploratory and not prespecified. The major aim is to establish matters of design, to try to establish what measures might be feasible, etc. The second phase is the evaluation proper which can now be prespecified with some hope of making sensible decisions.

Evaluation questions to do with process do not necessarily have to be prespecified in the same amount of detail. They tend to be addressed by using qualitative methods where there is a tradition of flexible design in which many aspects of the design, including the questions to which answers are sought, emerge during the process of data gathering. However, as Miles and Huberman (1994, p. 17) suggest 'Highly inductive, loosely designed studies make good sense when experienced researchers have plenty of time and are exploring exotic cultures, understudied phenomena, or very complex social phenomena'. How far each of these conditions applies in most small-scale evaluations could be debated, but it is highly unlikely you will have plenty of time. The proposal made here of prespecifying the evaluation questions obviously introduces a considerable degree of prespecification to the design which helps to make the task feasible. However, it does not preclude the possibility of some flexibility.

Again, there may be advantage in structuring the evaluation in two phases. In the first, you are effectively carrying the evaluation questions around with you and, opportunistically, getting a feel for how you might get answers to the questions. This can be followed by a more structured phase where you have made decisions about what kinds of sampling and data-collection methods are most efficient.

Doing a Shoe-String Evaluation

Anyone who has worked their way through the book to this point will appreciate that simply because an evaluation is small in scale does not mean it is simple and straightforward to carry out. However, there may well be situations where you are asked to do things on a shoe-string; in other words where time and other resources are very severely limited. The brief is, say, 'let us have a report in three weeks' time – and you are on your own'.

Whether you accept this offer or turn it down gracefully depends on a number of factors. You should be satisfied the 'standards' requirements discussed in Chapter 3 (Figure 3.1) can be met. In particular that there is likely to be:

- *utility* – is it going to be both useful and used? If they are pressing you like this, then indications are they want to use the findings;
- *feasibility* – can something worthwhile be done within the time and resources available?
- *propriety* – can the ethical aspects be fully and properly covered?
- *accuracy* – will you be able to provide adequate information for judgements about the program to be made?

The bottom line here is the ethical aspect. If you can't satisfy yourself on this you don't do it. Linked to it is the likely use of the evaluation, where you may well wish to steer clear of a 'pseudo-evaluation' (such as simply having an evaluation done because the rules say you must).

Obviously, the more experience you have of small-scale evaluations, the more likely you are to be able to deliver one on a shoe-string. This experience, and/or the inferior but still worthwhile appreciation of the issues involved through reading this book, should help in planning the use of your restricted time. At the minimum you need to:

- Establish the key question the evaluation is seeking to answer with the sponsor; and the nature of any report.
- Discuss the program and its evaluation with at least some of the key stakeholders. They help you to frame and design the study.
- Use data-collection methods which are feasible within the time available. For example you may have to restrict it to a short direct observation of the program in operation, a few interviews with key personnel and getting hold of as much existing documentation and records as possible. Assistance from others is great, but only if you can rely on it.
- Produce the agreed report, or other type of feedback, on time. It is crucial this is in a form and language which communicates with the audience(s) that will use the findings.

Chapter 5: Tasks

1. Review the set of evaluation questions you produced for task 4 in the previous chapter. Select what you consider to be the key questions.

   - Try to keep down the number of questions in the first instance. You may be able to consider additional ones, particularly if they are 'low cost' in terms of the resources needed to get relevant information (see below).

2. For any key question(s) concerning outcomes, consider what *measures* might be used to gather relevant information.

- Give suggestions for the thing to be measured (e.g. 'weight loss' after a slimming program) and how it might be operationalized (e.g. 'difference between weight on entry to the program and weights both immediately on completion and after three months').

3. For any key question(s) concerning process, consider what *methods* might be used to gather relevant information.

   - It may be feasible to gather information relevant to a question using more than one method (e.g. using both observation and semi-structured interviews) permitting cross-checking (triangulation).

4. For each question, consider how you will *sample* in terms of people, settings, occasions, times, etc.

5. Put this together for the set of key questions producing a *minimum plan* which shows what has to be done to gather the required information.

   - The format for this is up to you. One possibility is to do this as a 'time budget' as discussed in the following chapter.

6. Repeat 2–4 for the other evaluation questions and prefer a draft outline of the *full plan* which would be needed to gather information relevant to all the questions.

   - It is highly likely that this will turn out to be unrealistic given the time and resources you have available. The next chapter seeks to remedy this.

6
SOME PRACTICALITIES

This chapter deals with how you move from ideas and good intentions to actually getting the work done. It concentrates on the part of the evaluation where data and information are being gathered, and then analysed. Obviously the specific things to be done will vary substantially from one study to another. However, there are some general considerations common to virtually all evaluations. For example things almost always take longer than you think they will do. And it is highly likely the evaluation will upset some of the people involved. They may see sinister intentions very different from the laudable aims you have carefully agreed with the stakeholders. These are illustrations of two aspects worth serious consideration: realistic planning and relationships.

Time Budgeting

Chapter 5 was concerned with developing the central part of the evaluation plan: what you need to do to collect information which is going to help you get answers to the evaluation questions. It is highly desirable to get this translated into a time budget – i.e. a listing of planned activities and of the time and resources they will take up.

It makes sense to include everything in the time budget, right from your first involvement to the final completion of the evaluation. Depending on when you get round to making out this budget, some of the steps will already have been taken. Putting the known times these steps took, probably longer than you thought they would, into the budget may help you to be more realistic in your estimates for future times.

For the central part of the evaluation, where you are collecting information to answer the evaluation questions, you may find it helpful to structure the budget under the different questions. However, it is highly likely there will be overlap between the kinds of activity needed to gather information relevant to different questions, particularly those relating to process. Hence it may be preferable to structure according to activity, indicating the questions to which the activity is relevant. Figure 6.1 gives a pro-forma organized in this way.

It is a good idea to keep a copy of your initial version of this budget, and also to have a wall-chart or white-board version you can amend and

Phase	Activity		Responsibility	Date												
				Jan	Feb	Mar	Apr	May	Jun	Jul	Aug	Sep	Oct	Nov	Dec
Preparatory	1)														
	2)														
	3)														
	etc.														
Data gathering	Evaluation question(s)														
		1)													
		2)													
		3)													
		4)													
		etc.													
Analysis and reporting	1)														
	2)														
	3)														
	etc.														

Figure 6.1 *Sample time budget*

annotate as you go along, and then to compare the two at the end of the project, which might help to improve your time-budgeting skills for the future. It can also be of assistance in discussions of any divergences from the original plan, and explaining the reasons for these changes. If you keep a record of any changes as they occur, this provides a kind of trail documenting the development of the evaluation which could be used by others to audit it. In studies with an emergent design where it has been agreed it was inappropriate to prespecify fully the set of activities, such change is naturally expected. It is useful here to be able to establish the trail of evidence for decisions influencing the development of the study.

Looking at the totality of the evaluation in this way can help in anticipating possible road-blocks ahead. For example, approval from an ethics committee might have to be received before any direct involvement with participants can be started. Knowing the dates when the committee meets, and the likely time they will take to reach a decision, should help you to reschedule your activities to avoid wasting time. Permissions in general, such as getting clearance to work with vulnerable groups or in health-related or educational settings, can take a long time. This can be so even when the evaluation is sponsored by the same organization, particularly if the local setting is equivocal about a centrally sponsored study.

There is a tendency to think in an unnecessarily linear manner, assuming without thinking it through that one activity has to be completed before the next can be started. There is also a common inertia in moving from one phase to the next. Particularly when working in some 'field' setting, what was initially rather strange and threatening can become almost a second home in a surprisingly short space of time. Excuses may be found to prolong the involvement prior to moving on to something new.

What actually happens in an evaluation is likely to be more complex and messy than any plan suggests, but nevertheless it does help in time budgeting to separate out the various activities. A time budget is also very useful when you are placed in the difficult situation where the evaluation has to be completed and recommendations made by a given date if they are to be of any use – for example where items permitting the continuation or extension of a program have to be included in financial plans by that date. A realistic assessment of the time to completion may well indicate there is little chance of achieving this goal. This is one of the reasons for thinking in terms of a 'minimum plan' as suggested in the tasks linked to the previous chapter.

It may even be necessary to 'trade down' in design terms from this minimum plan – in other words renegotiating a simpler design which is still capable of giving some kind of answer to the key evaluation questions within the timescale. If this does not prove feasible, then there is little point in continuing. The situation to be avoided is that of carrying on regardless and then apologetically admitting at the due date there wasn't enough time to finish; or to cobble together conclusions for which you do not have real evidence. This doesn't help your sponsors or your reputation.

The time budget is also helpful when working out a financial budget for the evaluation. While each organization and funding body will have their own specific rules and conventions for budgeting, it is usual to have personnel and non-personnel budget headings or categories. As with time budgeting, there is a very common tendency to underestimate. If you are in a competitive tendering situation, there can be a temptation to try to undercut the others. There are some situations where it is more important to get the contract or grant and it may be possible to subsidise this particular evaluation in one way or another. However, 'loss-leaders' of this kind cannot be the norm, particularly if you are working on a commercial basis.

Certainly it is foolish deliberately to undertake an evaluation where you know the financial resources devoted to it are insufficient for you to do a good job.

Gaining Access

For many small-scale evaluations, gaining access is not an issue. The very fact that you have been asked to be involved as an evaluator gets you in. Or if you are carrying out an insider evaluation you are already there. However, there is access and access. Simply because there has been an agreement with a sponsor, probably with policy-makers and administrators having been party to it, doesn't mean others in the situation are going to welcome you.

Formally, the first step is to establish whether permission is going to be needed for your involvement. The initial points of contact which are set up when you are having discussions about the feasibility of the evaluation can probably give you the answer but you may need to use these contacts to suggest who else you need to approach.

Suppose for example you are asked to evaluate provision in a number of special units attached to a group of secondary schools. Perhaps the evaluation is being funded through a national initiative where a local education authority has been successful in its bid. Hopefully in a situation like this much of the spade-work will have been done by whoever put the bid together. The various schools and units will have agreed to be involved and may have assisted in actually shaping the bid. Even in a highly favourable situation like this where there is effectively an 'in principle' existing agreement to participate, it may not be plain sailing. Inevitably time will have passed. The schools and units may now have other priorities. Staff may have changed. Tensions may have developed between local authority and school, or between schools and units. While you ought to be able to rely on the good offices of the group responsible for the bid, it is likely to be your task to renegotiate access. It may well be the case that the actual evaluation will be more important to you than anyone in the schools or units (they should be concerned about the program or service forming the subject of the evaluation, but that doesn't necessarily lead to them being favourably disposed to the evaluation).

Less favourable situations could raise formidable access problems. Suppose an administrator, perhaps feeling these units were not functioning effectively, secured funding to evaluate them. He might have the power to get you in to the settings under his control but it is questionable whether you would get a favourable reception when inside. The same kinds of issues could well arise at a more micro level when access is being negotiated in within-school units.

There is an important distinction between what is needed formally to gain access and what needs to happen to gain the support and acceptance of those involved. Local knowledge of the organization or other setting, whether obtained directly by your own observation or vicariously by discussions with contacts who are themselves knowledgeable, will help you to identify important 'gate-keepers'. These are people in positions of authority or influence. Those with influence may not necessarily having formal positions of authority. Managers, head and deputy head-teachers, and ward sisters fall in the first category. Those who have influence on whether you and the evaluation are going to be favourably received, based on something other than formal authority, will obviously vary from one organization to another. Likely candidates include the teacher who has been there for many years or a similarly experienced secretary.

At first sight it might seem the 'insider' evaluator is not likely to have access problems. Within large organizations there may be a separate group with evaluation and related responsibilities. When their evaluation task focuses on some other part of the organization, they may find their situation is not all that different from that of an outsider. No doubt the formal arrangement of access can be easily done, although even in this respect power struggles and old animosities may queer the pitch. However, gaining access in the sense of active support and acceptance could be very problematic, particularly if there is something of a history of previous evaluations having led to what are regarded as unfortunate or unfair outcomes.

Certainly insiders should have the advantage of an intimate knowledge of the organization both in terms of its formal structures and of the influential gate-keepers. They are also likely to have an understanding of the setting in historical and developmental perspective which it is very difficult for an outsider to appreciate.

For the real insider, say the practitioner or professional who has agreed to take an evaluative role focusing on some aspect of the setting in which they work, or have worked, the situation has quite sharp negative and positive features. On the positive side, you will know the setting well in both formal and informal aspects. You know what the jobs there entail and what really happens when people do them. Assuming one of the reasons you have been selected to help do the evaluation is that you were good at the job, then you will have 'street credibility' with your colleagues.

More negatively, it may be difficult to take on this new role, and there may well be jealousies and antagonism from those you have worked with. There can be problems of status differential, particularly in hierarchical organizations. Someone formerly (or formally) at a higher level than you may not take kindly to your working in the role of evaluator, which is rather difficult to classify in hierarchical terms. If the evaluation, for whatever reason, does not go well, then this can make lasting problems if you stay in the same organization. If the findings are not utilized, this puts you in a difficult position. If they are used to make unpopular changes then guess who will be blamed! From the point of view of carrying out a high-quality evaluation, you are likely to find it very difficult to stand back from the situation sufficiently to be able to take an unbiased and unprejudiced view of something you know well.

I hope the picture painted above is not so bleak it puts off all potential insider evaluators. Figure 6.2 gives some suggestions for coping with this situation.

Getting Organized

You will need to have an operationalized version of the time budget – i.e. something which works out in as much detail as you can what you

---

1) *Use your knowledge of the situation and people involved to try to foresee likely problems and conflicts.* For example there may be conflicts between the behaviour appropriate to any other role you have in the organization and your role as evaluator. Or you may know a particular person may be likely to subvert the evaluation perhaps because of personal animosity, or of insecurity.

2) *Work out a plan to deal with them.* You may have to differentiate your roles so you are an evaluator at certain times or in particular situations and, say, a personnel officer at other times or situations. Generally knowledge is power and you ought to be able to work something out. Your sponsor, or whoever you report to in the organization in respect of the evaluation, should give you any necessary support, but it will be as well to have thought through likely difficulties and raised the issues before taking on the evaluation.

3) *Keep a full record of your interactions in the situation, either in your evaluation diary or elsewhere.* Subsequent reflection on this log outside the situation should help in getting an objective assessment of any possible contaminating effects of your insider status on what you have seen and recorded.

4) *Have a colleague with evaluation experience who you can discuss problems and issues with OUTSIDE THE SETTING OF THE EVALUATION (i.e. both the colleague and the discussions to be outside the setting).* This kind of support is invaluable in maintaining your morale and sanity. It will also help with the quality of the study. You should clear this relationship with the sponsor and other key stakeholders to cover possible ethical issues.

Figure 6.2 *Coping as an 'insider' evaluator*
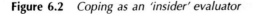

are doing and when and where you are doing it. The extent to which an evaluation can be spelled out in detail beforehand depends very much on the style of the evaluation. However, even with a very flexible design where later activities depend on how the earlier ones work out, it should be feasible to have tentative timed and sequenced lists of these various activities.

In practice there are often fixed deadlines which have to be met, particularly if the hope and intention is that findings will be utilized. These deadlines concentrate the mind wonderfully. You may find that whereas the plan was to allow for two weeks for a set of interviews, by really getting your skates on they could be completed in two days. And whereas it was the intention to get them transcribed and fully analysed, you may be able to get what you need from them by simply listening to the tapes and selecting key comments so that the time for this is drastically reduced. Then burning the midnight oil gets the interim report in just in time for the meeting which decides whether phase two of the project is going to go ahead!

An important part of being organized is the keeping of commitments. If you say you will be at the clinic, or school, or wherever at 9am on Tuesday morning, be there. And if you can't because some emergency has cropped up, then make sure a message gets through to everybody you were going to see. If the word gets around you are unreliable and/or disorganized, it will very quickly be almost impossible to rescue the situation. In many evaluations the participants do find the situation somewhat aversive and they need little encouragement to write the whole thing off as a waste of their time; so don't give them any excuse to view it in that negative light. You should also reconfirm any arrangements you make for visits or other involvements before turning up. Simply because a letter was sent to your contact person in the organization some time ago by no means guarantees your visit will be expected.

It is, of course, possible to get into a positive, virtuous spiral. Providing the early encounters go well, and the organization of any meetings is impeccable, etc., then any initial misgivings will be allayed. Their feeling of having coped well may then rebound to your, and the evaluation's, advantage.

This is not simply a matter of organization. Your approach and general demeanour send important verbal and non-verbal messages to everyone involved. If you are tense, or bored, or have prejudices against them, or appear to behave differently to the generals as against the troops, then you can be sure it will affect how you are reacted to. Generally, your relationships do influence the quality of the data you will gather and it is worth working on your social skills to ensure you are not handicapping yourself unnecessarily. The underlying assumption is you are entering into the evaluation in good faith, that it appears to you it is an ethical enterprise carried out for worthy purposes, and hence there is nothing wrong with a whole-hearted commitment to it on your part.

Analysing the Data

Even a small small-scale evaluation can generate a surprisingly large amount of data. Interviews and questionnaires may well produce many words, with some of them perhaps hidden away in audio-tapes. Your harvest of documents about the planning and running of the program can lead to many more. Similarly relevant records may provide you with much data in numerical form, as will most assessments of program outcomes.

Your task is to make some sense of all this. The most important initial task is to make yourself familiar with what you have and how it might be used to answer your evaluation questions. This is not a one-off task which you leave until near the end of the evaluation process. Right from the start you should be keeping tabs on what data you have in the bag and thinking what you might do to cover any gaps. Many small-scale evaluations are, at least partly, exploratory and it is not feasible to preplan everything. Some of the data you collect because it seemed a good idea at the time may have to be jettisoned because things developed differently from what you first thought. Simply because you have data doesn't mean you have to analyse it; although, obviously, as a busy person you want to get out of blind alleys where you are collecting data which are not going to be useful as soon as possible.

Broadly speaking, data can be thought of as either *quantitative* (numbers, or easily turned into numbers) or *qualitative* (almost always in the form of words). Their treatment is in many ways quite different, but the overall principle in both cases is you first check and in some way 'code' the data, then you seek to analyse and interpret.

Quantitative Data

The analysis of quantitative data is a huge and complex topic. Fortunately, however, even though a small-scale evaluation may generate large amounts of data in the form of numbers, it is rarely necessary to do anything complicated with them. The main exception is when you have used an experimental design as part of an outcome evaluation. Here, as discussed in Chapter 4, there is likely to be a strong expectation you report the statistical significance of differences between groups. To do this an appropriate statistical test has to be used. If you already have the requisite skills, this is not a problem. If you don't then you must seek the assistance of someone who does. Incidentally, you need this advice at the design stage of the evaluation to ensure the kind and amount of data you are proposing to collect are capable of analysis. Otherwise Murphy's law is highly likely to operate once more, in the form that leaving decisions on statistical analysis to the end leads to unanalysable data.

Using computer packages for statistical analysis. The carrying out of statistical analysis is greatly facilitated by the use of computer packages, of which SPSS (Statistical Package for the Social Sciences) is probably the most widely used (Bryman and Cramer, 1997; Foster, 1998). While their use is not particularly difficult, doing this without statistical experience or help is not recommended. It is all too easy to produce impressive-looking nonsense.

Coding quantitative data. Some initially non-numerical data can be turned into numbers easily. If data are collected in a structured way as in a questionnaire with fixed-choice answers it is straightforward to code these answers. All that is required is to give the same symbol (usually a number) to each of the possible answers. This helps in using databases or similar computer packages. Thus for a yes/no/don't know answer the coding might be:

Yes	1
No	2
Don't know	3
No response	4

The actual number given to each answer is, of course, arbitrary. Once coded, the frequency of each answer (i.e. the number of times it occurs) can be worked out.

Some fixed-choice answers yield more meaningful numbers – e.g. 'extremely so/very much so/quite a bit/some/a little/not at all' might be coded '5/4/3/2/1/0' respectively. There is still a degree of arbitrariness in the particular numbers assigned, but it is reasonable to view higher numbers as indicating more positive answers. Again it will be necessary to code 'no response' separately, though its coding would be arbitrary (say with a letter, such as n; or with a number not otherwise used, say '9' – in the latter case it would be necessary to ensure that the 9s do not get counted in when working out totals or averages).

It is not at all straightforward to do this kind of coding when dealing with open-ended answers as obtained in semi-structured interviews, or the 'Any other comments you would like to make?' question sometimes added after fixed-choice questions in a questionnaire. From study of the answers given, you may be able to come up with a set of categories into which most of them fall and then assign codes to each of these categories. This approach is an aspect of *content analysis* and can be time-consuming even for those with previous experience as it is necessary to demonstrate the reliability of the categories in a way similar to that called for in a structured observation schedule. To avoid some of these difficulties, it is preferable, when you wish to work with quantitative data, to ensure you present fixed-choice questions with preset categories. There will still be difficulties in establishing these categories but the work will have been done up-front and sorted out prior to analysis. The alternative is to stick with the words produced by such questions, and analyse them as qualitative data, as discussed below.

Summarizing and displaying quantitative data. For most small-scale evaluations, the main task after any quantitative data have been assembled and coded is to find ways of describing and displaying what you have got. Typically you will have columns of numbers in some kind of table which may be adequate to do this. However, it is easy to get lost when there is anything more than very small amounts of data.

Providing simple summaries in the form of totals and means (averages) helps considerably. These are known as *descriptive statistics*, and there are several others (for example, medians and modes) which may be preferable to means in some circumstances. It can also be of interest to provide information about the variability of the scores in sets of data (measured, for example, by the variance or standard deviation). Robson (1994) provides a simple account of the meaning and computation of such statistics.

Even more useful than this is the graphical display of your data. Graphs, bar-charts and pie-charts are now very easy to generate using the facilities included with many computer packages including popular word processors. Figure 6.3 provides a set of possibilities, to which the use of colour for greater effect could be added. Their use is pretty self-evident, apart from, perhaps, the 'bubble chart'. Here the size of the circle (or bubble) represents the values of a third variable, additional to those on the horizontal and vertical axes. Henry (1997) covers a wide range of ways of displaying quantitative data, which can be thought of not only as a part of their analysis but also as a powerful means of communicating your findings.

Summarizing and displaying quantitative data are of considerable help in answering your evaluation questions. Provided they are closely linked to these questions, the data very largely speak for themselves. If attendance figures at three schools where a truancy program has been in operation rise from averages of 67, 75 and 76% to 88, 90 and 87% respectively, then this provides good evidence for the success of the program. You may be able to provide more convincing evidence by setting this in the context of the previous three years where there have been gradually worsening attendance figures. Or if similar schools in the area where the program has not been in operation show no corresponding improvement.

As indicated in the section on experimental design in Chapter 4, while some might hanker for information about whether or not such changes are 'statistically significant' (and if this is important for your sponsor or other key stakeholders, by all means provide this, if necessary getting statistical help) it only tells you whether the changes are unlikely to have happened by chance. Note this kind of analysis does not in itself provide evidence about whether any improvement is attributable to the program itself. To answer that question convincingly by means of an experimental design by itself would probably call for some kind of randomized assignment to experimental schools where the program ran and control schools where it didn't. Even that would be open to the criticism that it was the extra resources represented by the presence of the program staff,

or some other linked feature, rather than the program itself which caused
the change. More sophisticated designs could tease out some of these
confounding factors, but this then gets well beyond the possible for a
small-scale evaluation.

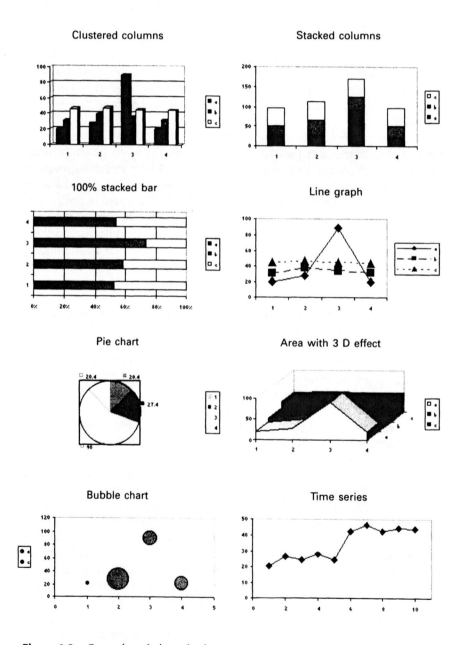

Figure 6.3 *Examples of chart displays*

So, to reiterate, in a simple small study, the priority is to summarize and display the evidence you have garnered relevant to the program outcomes or other evaluation questions. You make the best case you can, buttressed by contextual supporting evidence from whatever data sources you have available.

Cross-tabulation and subgroup analyses. A simple mean or average score is usually the most obvious quantitative index relevant to deciding whether an objective has been achieved, or more generally what is the answer to an evaluation question. Another common interest is in the possible relationship between scores on different variables. Do girls or boys show greater improvement in school attendance following the program? Or, are there differences between pupils from different ethnic backgrounds? Table 6.1 shows the type of 'contingency table' which can be used to illustrate possible relationships. It is good practice to include both actual numbers (the 'frequencies') as well as percentages. Here the interest is likely to be in the differing gender ratios in different schools and hence column percentages would be used. In other situations row percentages might be more relevant.

This is another situation where the conventional approach is to assess the statistical significance of the apparent relationship; in other words its likelihood of having occurred by chance. Exactly the same arguments apply as in the previous section. Even if it is accepted that an apparently interesting relationship is worth following up, with or without the benefit of significance testing, it must be appreciated there are many possible interpretations of such a relationship. Certainly one cannot assume a causal relationship (in either direction!) without other supporting findings. A link to theory may be one way of increasing its plausibility.

Instead of focusing on relationships, it is possible to think of this in terms of differences between subgroups, as originally expressed when asking whether boys and girls show different outcomes. This is useful

Table 6.1 *Examples of contingency tables*

Observed frequencies (i.e. numbers of children)

	School 1	School 2	School 3	School 4	School 5	Totals
Female	24	30	12	2	16	84
Male	24	22	8	34	28	116
Totals	48	52	20	36	44	200

Percentages of row totals

	School 1	School 2	School 3	School 4	School 5	Totals
Female	28.6	35.7	14.3	2.4	19.0	100
Male	20.7	19.0	6.9	29.3	24.1	100
Totals	24	26	10	18	22	100

Percentages of column totals

	School 1	School 2	School 3	School 4	School 5	Totals
Female	50	57.7	60	5.6	36.4	42
Male	50	42.3	40	94.4	63.6	58
Totals	100	100	100	100	100	100

Table 6.2   *Example of a subgroup approach*

| | Relative improvement shown by | |
Intensity of involvement with program	'Disadvantaged prisoners'	'Maximum security' prisoners
Below average	27%	–09%
Average	54%	27%
Intense	52%	43%
Very intense	20%	87%

Source: Pawson and Tilley (1997, p. 112, Table 4.7, part only)

when seeking to establish for whom a program works best and under which circumstances. Table 6.2 provides an example.

Qualitative Data

The basic task is to understand what you have got. The data are telling you something; your task is to work out what that is. The task is complicated by the fact there is no single agreed way of doing this. There are many different strategies associated with different theoretical conceptualizations of the research task. Coffey and Atkinson (1996) provide a very helpful overview for those who wish to take this further.

In small-scale evaluations, it may well be adequate simply to regard the task as one of categorization, establishing what some refer to as *themes*. Essentially you are trying to establish what the data tell you relating to the evaluation questions. You may be faced simply with one source of qualitative data, such as a set of tapes or transcripts from some interviews. It is more likely you will have several sources, perhaps including notes from observation and documents as well as different types of interview. In this case, you can cross-check or *triangulate* the information obtained from the different sources. To the extent that the same categories or themes seem to be appropriate, you gain greater confidence you are on to something.

This is a kind of *coding* exercise. However, it differs from the coding discussed in connection with the analysis of quantitative data where the object was to generate numbers which could be added, averaged or otherwise subjected to statistical analysis. Here you are trying to identify parts of observational notes or interview transcripts as in some way similar, perhaps indicative of a theme or relevant to a particular question. Its frequent occurrence may suggest it is important. However, something which is only picked up once or twice, but which appears particularly striking or revealing, could be well worth following up.

This illustrates two linked aspects of an evaluation which is making substantial use of techniques yielding qualitative data. First, that the data analysis should not wait upon the completion of data collection but should be ongoing. Preliminary analyses will reveal tentative evidence about possible ways of looking at the data. Secondly, the flexibility of 'qualitative' designs usually means that it is possible to collect additional data (e.g. by interviewing more people, or observing at a different time or place) to further corroborate or contradict the emerging patterns of evidence.

As the analysis and the evaluation continue, when you have got on top of the mound of qualitative data and have a good understanding of what it contains, you should be able to firm up on the important categories. They may need modification to take on board insights which come to you, or contradictory evidence which must be taken note of.

Where do the themes come from? While they can come from all kinds of sources, it may be helpful to highlight two particular ones: *emergent* and *theory based*. In situations where you are in an exploratory mode (perhaps at an early stage of involvement with a program you know little about), possible themes may emerge from your study of data such as notes you make from observation, or records of informal interviews. This derivation of emergent themes is consonant with so-called 'grounded theory', a popular approach within social science research first advocated by Glaser and Strauss (1967). See Strauss and Corbin (1999) for a more practically orientated discussion of its use.

In small-scale evaluations it is likely you go into the situation with quite well developed notions of what you are looking for and occasions where themes emerge in this pure way are rare. Also evaluations are notoriously conducted under time pressure making the kind of prolonged exposure to the situation usually considered necessary an expensive luxury.

In very general terms, the themes you bring into the situation can be thought of as theory based. In the language we developed in Chapter 4, they derive from the hunches, guesses or hypotheses about the mechanisms which may be operating.

Using computer packages for qualitative data analysis. There are several packages available which can undoubtedly improve the quality of your analysis. Weitzman and Miles (1995) review many of them, covering those best adapted to specific tasks. The most widely used which is adaptable to many of the tasks involved in analysing these data is known as NUD.IST – Non-numerical, Unstructured Data Indexing, Searching and Theorizing (Gahan and Hannibal, 1998). In essence, they do little more than can be achieved by the traditional craft skills of annotating multiple photocopies, using multicoloured highlighters, scissors and paste in order to put together the various bits relating to a theme. However, they do help in keeping track of all the coding you have done and of knowing where everything is. They also facilitate making linkages between themes and changing and developing the various themes as you proceed.

The main problem is that it undoubtedly takes time and effort to be able to use a package efficiently. Also it is not really feasible to hand over the task to a specialist in the way you can with statistical analysis. Your own perceptions and judgement still play a central role in the coding process. It may be feasible to persuade a colleague, or someone helping with the evaluation, who either has the requisite skills or is willing to acquire them, to work alongside you in this task. Otherwise, unless you are likely to find these skills useful in the future, it is probably not worth while to spend the time on this simply for one small-scale evaluation. Do it by hand; there are still advocates of this approach as they feel it keeps them closer to the data.

Chapter 6: Tasks

1. Complete a time budget for your evaluation:

    *   The level of detail is up to you; the most important thing is to try to be as realistic as possible in your estimation.
    *   Modify it as necessary as the evaluation proceeds.

2. Use the time budget to prepare an analysis of the costs involved in the evaluation.

    *   It may well be this has to be prepared at the beginning of the process in order to secure a contract or agreement to carry out the evaluation. This causes difficulties in that it has been argued the design should be developed collaboratively with the sponsor and key stakeholders. It may be feasible to have sufficient initial inter-action with them to do this. If not you do the best you can; and prepare for changes as you get involved.

3. Ensure you have negotiated the access required to carry out the various activities of the evaluation.

    *   The collaboration you have established with key stakeholders should stand you in good stead.

4. Carry out the evaluation in as professional and organized way as you can manage.

    *   Remember all evaluations are sensitive.

5. For any quantitative data to be collected, ensure access to SPSS or similar computer package, and that you or available others have the skills to use it. Arrange to buy in support if essential.

6. For any qualitative data decide whether you are going to use NUD.IST or a similar equivalent computer package. The decision depends on the skills available to you and amount of data likely to be gathered.

7
COMMUNICATING THE FINDINGS

Evaluation Reports

There are no hard and fast rules for the way in which the findings of small-scale evaluations are communicated. The ideas of *audience* and *purpose* are important; who are you seeking to communicate with, and why? There can be multiple audiences and multiple purposes. It is highly likely that one audience will be the sponsor of the evaluation, but key stakeholders including program personnel and, possibly, clients may be others. One purpose will probably be to fulfil the terms of any contract or formal agreement (which may have specified the kind of reporting required). Similarly, undertakings about feedback made to anyone involved should be honoured. Another purpose might be to facilitate implementation of the findings.

Emphasizing the multifaceted nature of the communication task makes it clear you might have to cover this in a number of ways. The most common form of communication is the *evaluation report,* and it may be that different styles of report are needed for different audiences or purposes. Or that a full report goes to one audience, and perhaps parts only to others.

The Formal Written Report

The format of this report is a matter for negotiation between yourself and its main audience, usually the sponsor or the decision-maker with prime responsibility for implementing any findings. They are likely to be busy people and so to maximize the chances they will read it and act upon it, it should be clearly written and professionally presented. Executive summaries (one page preferably, and at the front of the report) are needed. Figure 7.1 gives an example of a possible structure. Whatever structure is used, the report should be written in a language that speaks to the policy people or whoever constitute the audience. Charts, diagrams and graphs are invaluable in communicating findings. They should be self-explanatory with all necessary information included in the display and its heading (see, for example, Tufte, 1983; Henry, 1997). Simple tables with totals, averages and percentages, where appropriate, can also convey much information economically.

Heading
Make it short and clear. Add a subheading to amplify if necessary. Avoid clever or jokey headings, they tend to trivialize or not communicate well.

Table of contents
Simple list of main headings and page numbers. Don't include subheadings.

Executive summary
The most important part for first-time readers and busy executives. Summary of key findings and conclusions/recommendations. Limit each point to a short paragraph, including a relevant fact or example. Single page preferable; not more than two.

Background
One-page scene-setter outlining why the study was carried out, what questions you are seeking answers to and why the findings are likely to be of interest.

Approach taken
Short description of when, where and how the study was carried out (e.g. methods used; who was involved). Put detailed descriptions and specialist information into appendices.

Findings
Largest section giving your answers to the evaluation questions; needs careful ordering and structuring. Put the main message at the beginning. Signpost main findings with headings. Use subheadings to highlight subsidiary points or break up long text passages.

Conclusions/recommendations
Draws together main themes of the report and (most importantly) their implications. If recommendations are included structure clearly using bullet points.

Appendices
Include any information which is needed by the audience to understand or substantiate material in the main report (e.g. references, technical details). Do them on coloured paper; it emphasizes that the main report is quite short. Not a dumping ground for other material you happen to have but which they don't need.

NB   Include names, addresses, telephones, faxes and emails for evaluator(s).

Figure 7.1   *Possible structure of an evaluation report*

While it has been argued at several points in this book that theory has an important role in guiding an evaluation and understanding the working of a program, it may be politic to avoid the use of the 't' word in many reports. What you do need to include in discussing the findings and coming to conclusions or recommendations are the fruits of your use of theory. If there is evidence for the operation of one or more mechanisms in leading to favourable outcomes (or other mechanisms blocking such outcomes) this can be indicated in a way which does not require mention of theory. Or if it appears the implementation of aspects of the program was faulty or inadequate, such that there has not been a fair test of the ideas underlying the program, this should also be stressed.

Alternative reports. It may be feasible to use the same report for more than one audience. Or rephrasing the executive summary, or other short parts of the report, may be all that is needed. However, for some audiences it is best to start again. For example, reporting back to parents who have taken part in a school parental involvement program may be best done by something like a four-page small-format newsletter. Take care, though, that the text and presentation do communicate to the target audience; condescending oversimplification is at least as bad as barely understandable jargon.

There are alternatives to reports. An oral presentation might communicate more effectively with busy administrators. It provides you with an opportunity to seize their attention, quite possibly for substantially longer than the time they would give to something in their in-tray. This also calls for professional standards, both in your verbal input and any visual aids such as overhead projector transparencies. Similarly with accompanying handouts, which would include your executive summary. Discussions at such meetings can be more profitable if you have had prior talks with those likely to influence the way in which the presentation is received.

Other possibilities include posters, video-tapes and web pages. The same rules apply; make sure they are done to a high professional standard, getting design help if possible.

Who owns the report? This should have been settled, preferably in writing, in the initial agreement between you and the sponsor. If it goes out under your name, then it should be something you can live with in the sense that it fulfils ethical guidelines. It is not unreasonable for the sponsor to see a draft version and to ask for changes, particularly when the findings are critical. Providing any such changes do not distort the findings and are essentially presentational or factual (where you agree you got it wrong) then you should keep the sponsor happy by accepting them. Remember you are interested in the findings being acted on, and this is unlikely to happen when they are being contested. If there has been a continuing involvement with the sponsor and key stakeholders, they should feel some degree of ownership of the evaluation and it is unlikely the findings will come as a major shock to them.

Academic reports. There is much to be said in favour of reporting your evaluation findings to academic or professional audiences. This should, however, be thought of as a secondary audience. Your prime audience is to the sponsor or key stakeholders in the program. Holding fast to this primary target keeps you honest in the sense of focused on the purposes and questions you have agreed with them. However, producing an academically or professionally orientated account keeps you honest in a rather different way. There will be a focus on technical adequacy both of the evaluation itself, and the way in which it is reported.

This type of reporting is also a major way in which there can be cumulation and improvement, both in evaluation methodology and also in the substantive fields covered by social programs. While the notion of the 'experimenting society' (Campbell, 1969), or that programs and services should always fulfil evidenced-based criteria, may seem distantly Utopian, these kinds of publications help in making modest moves in such a direction.

Concern for audience is equally important in this context. Different journals, both academic and professional, tend to have very specific requirements in terms of format, style and length of contribution. These are either stated explicitly or can be induced from contributions in recent issues. Conference presentations, either direct or through poster sessions, can offer a useful niche for reporting small studies. The reporting of small-scale evaluations as part of the requirements for university or other courses is also likely to have detailed guidelines. It is sensible if such guidelines permit the incorporation of the primary evaluation report (i.e. as prepared for the sponsor or other key stakeholders).

As with the internal report, your initial agreement with the sponsor should have clarified whether you can publish the evaluation and its findings in this way. Some organizations may require they can effectively veto this, and if so you should decide before starting whether you are prepared to work under such conditions.

Sexist or racist language in reports. Whichever type of report you produce, you should be sensitive to possible sexist or racist language. Various organizations have produced relevant guidelines (e.g. British Sociological Association, 1989a; 1989b).

Facilitating the Implementation of Evaluation Findings

An evaluation whose findings are not used in some way is close to a waste both of your time and the time of everyone else involved. Making it more likely they will be used is in large measure dependent on the way the evaluation has been set up and conducted. The whole emphasis in this book has been to carry out the evaluation in collaboration with key stakeholders so that they not only have a stake in the program, but also a stake in the evaluation and in the use of its findings.

Timing of the Report

A part of the planning of an evaluation should include the timing for presentation of the evaluation report. It is obviously sensible if this can be arranged so the report is available when decisions have to be made about the program. Organizations tend to work to fixed yearly timetables such that if crucial deadlines are not met then opportunities for action may be delayed or lost. If this is the case then it is obviously important you keep to any agreed timing.

If, as is not uncommon, problems occur (hopefully ones out of your control rather than due to your inefficiency) which look likely to lead to delay, then it is highly desirable the situation gets discussed as soon as possible. While a later date might be negotiated, it may be preferable to curtail some aspects of the evaluation so that the planned date can be met.

Being Realistic about Implementation

Small-scale evaluations probably stand a better chance of their findings being used than grander initiatives. They tend to be closer to the program and the people who make decisions about implementation. The questions to which they seek answers are usually relatively modest and the short timescale of small local evaluations helps to ensure relevant information is available in time for it to be useful. In particular, it is probably easier to run small-scale evaluations in a participative manner which creates the kind of atmosphere where implementation becomes expected by all concerned. You, as an evaluator, can have the kind of intimate involvement which, while it causes its own problems, undoubtedly helps to generate that atmosphere.

Nevertheless, there is no inevitability about the use of even the best designed and run evaluation. The context may change – in important personnel, or in the tasks and priorities of the organization, or in a myriad other ways. This can be to some extent insured against by being selective in where you get involved, going for those situations where the chances of stability appear favourable. Remember evaluation findings are but one of many influences in complex social situations. Even when there is little evidence of direct implementation a well conducted study may have other, wider, influences. Particularly with participative evaluative styles, program personnel and key stakeholders may be empowered to work in more reflective ways and, possibly, to incorporate a general questioning evaluative stance into their way of working. This links to what Weiss (1989) has referred to as the 'enlightenment' function of evaluation. That is the development of a general increase in understanding:

> people learn more about what happens in the program and afterwards. They gain a better idea of program strengths, fault lines, opportunities for improvement. Old myths are punctured, issues previously unrecognized come to the fore. As a result, people think differently . . . Although they may not *do* anything different for a while, the shift in thinking can in time have important consequences for the eventual actions they take.
>
> (Weiss, 1998, p. 317)

And, at the very least, you will have learned from the experience and will, hopefully, be armed to carry out more effective future evaluations.

Chapter 7: Tasks

1. Agree the format of the main report with the sponsor and other key stakeholders.

    - Discussion on this should have been part of the initial agreement (also issues of ownership, etc.).

2.   Decide on possible additional forms of reporting.

3.   Reflect on the whole exercise, and list five (or so) points you have
     learned which will make your next evaluation better.

Postscript

Two quotations from one of the earliest, and wisest, evaluators, Lee J.
Cronbach (1982, p. 335):

> no one learns to plan and conduct evaluations from a book. The way to learn
> is to try and try again, part of the time under circumstances where a more
> experienced practitioner can comment on the plans and suggestions that
> emerge from early data. . .

and

> no one ever learns all there is to know about evaluating; each experience
> teaches some new lesson. And, on the other hand, the intelligent beginner can
> make a welcome contribution. Handed an evaluation task for which no one
> in the organization is particularly well qualified, the novice finds it easy to
> produce data that stimulate thought and open up possibilities. The evaluator
> is in many cases the only person free to roam nearly everywhere and talk to
> nearly everyone, and so he can form a picture of the situation available to no
> one else. Using that opportunity tactfully requires maturity rather than
> expertise.

Advice which is difficult to better, beyond hoping and expecting that both
female and male evaluators now get in on the act.

APPENDIX A: NEEDS ANALYSIS

The view that public services are essentially about meeting needs is increasingly common. Manufacturers and business depend on specifying a need for a product or service, and then set about meeting that need. This appendix focuses on the analysis of needs as an initial step in the development of a program or service whose effectiveness is to be evaluated. For more general treatments of the topic see Percy-Smith (1996), who links needs assessment to public policy, and Baldwin (1998), who develops the topic in the context of community care.

An evaluator may be called upon to help assess the need for a proposed program. Or, even before the notion of the program is well developed, there may be a request to assess the needs of some group, say the homeless in a particular town, with a view to providing them with a service of some kind. This can provide an opportunity for the voices and perceptions of potential clients and disempowered groups to be heard. But these evaluative tasks are not without their own difficulties and dangers. As Guba and Lincoln (1989, p. 52) point out, the information gained can be used against the group from which it is solicited: 'Needs assessments too often identify just those needs that the sponsor's product happens to be capable of fulfilling, to which the sponsor happens to be capable of providing a response, or which the sponsor's values dictate ought to exist as needs of the target group.' However, approaching the task in good faith, and being sensitive to such further disempowering, provides some protection. In particular using the systematic approaches required by research will help you to make explicit the biases and values present and minimise their effect.

Defining Need

McKillip (1987) has provided a clear account of need analysis giving greater detail than possible here (see also McKillip, 1998). Using his terminology: a *need* is a *value judgment* that some *group* has a *problem* that can be *solved*. That is, the *value judgment* indicates a preference for a particular goal. A particular target group of people in specific circumstances have the *need*. A *problem* is an outcome which is in some way inadequate; where there is a difference between how things are and how it is felt they should or could be. *Solutions* indicate what might be done to 'solve' the problem, i.e. to get rid of that difference.

Behind such simple statements lies great complexity. For example, the inadequacy referred to is felt or expressed by someone. There are many possible sources of the feelings. *Felt need* is the target group's own preference. While there is a good case for giving primacy to their views, it may well appear to an impartial observer that conditions are clearly inadequate, even when no dissatisfaction is expressed. Suppose for example that circumstances are identified which predict poor outcomes, say a lack of qualifications or refusal to take up training opportunities. If support systems or allowances are changed, perhaps in the context of 'welfare to work' initiatives, then needs may be revealed which can't be articulated currently by the target group.

The way in which a problem is conceptualized has great influence on what appears to be appropriate as a solution (Seidman and Rappoport, 1986). Viewing the homeless as low-income persons with no family members to whom they can turn for support suggests solutions aiming to reduce social isolation. Defining homelessness as lack of access to conventional shelter suggests making available affordable and accessible housing. Berk and Rossi (1990, p. 39) develop this argument and provide further examples.

Carrying out a Need Analysis

Figure A.1 suggests a series of steps in carrying out an analysis of needs. As with other such attempts to reconstruct complex processes rationally, it should only be viewed as a broad framework and an aide-mémoire of aspects that need considering along the way.

Methods and Techniques for Assessing Need

Suggestions for possible methods and techniques are discussed below. Further details of their use are given in Chapter 5. The assessment of need is a particular kind of evaluative task and, as such, the general principles covered in this text apply. The methods you use depend on the specific questions about needs to which you seek answers, and on practical resource constraints. As indicated in step 5 of Figure A.1, multiple data-collection techniques are typically employed. Some possibilities are covered in Figure A.2.

Group techniques. A simple and efficient technique is to gather together an appropriate group and ask them to identify needs. What constitutes an 'appropriate' group is, however, problematic. An obvious candidate is the target group whose needs are being assessed. Alternatives include 'experts' who can draw upon experience with the population and knowledge of existing services and programs.

Specific techniques worth considering are:

• *Focus Groups* which are discussed in Chapter 5; and
• *Public Meetings* – which aren't; and so will be dealt with here.

1) *Identifying Users.* The users are both those who will act on the need analysis, and those who might be affected by it. Knowing each constituency helps in focusing the analysis and, subsequently, in having recommendations adopted.
2) *Identifying Uses.* Again helps to focus on how the problem is best conceptualized and what might count as a solution.
3) *Describing the Target Population.* Who and where they are, specified in terms of relevant characteristics (e.g. social indicators). How many? For existing programs, comparisons between users and non-users may reveal barriers or unmet needs.
4) *Describing the Context.* What is the physical and social environment of the program? Are there gaps in existing provision? Could existing provision be adopted or adapted?
5) *Identifying Need.* Description of problems of the target population. Suggestion of possible solution(s) and analysis of their likely effectiveness, feasibility and utilization. What are current outcomes and how might they be improved? This process typically involves the use of different sources of information and methods of data collection.
6) *Meeting Need.* Recommendations for action based on the needs, problems and solutions identified.
7) *Communicating Results and Recommendations.* As in any evaluation or applied research where implementation is an important aim, this is a crucial stage. A range of audiences will need to be catered for including decision-makers and potential users.

Note: The process is likely to be more complex than indicated by the orderly sequence given. Analysis is likely to throw up thoughts about further problems and/or solutions, which may call for further data gathering, etc. Communicating with audiences is likely, if time and resources permit (and it is highly desirable to budget for this), to take you back to the drawing board, and a further iteration through the steps.

Figure A.1 *Steps in need analysis*
Source: Adapted from McKillip (1998, pp. 264-5).

Public Meetings. Public meetings, or community groups, could be run according to focus group principles. However, focus groups work best when they are homogeneous and the central point of a community group is that all constituents (and constituencies) are represented. For many communities this is a recipe for heterogeneity rather than homogeneity.

There have been attempts to codify the organization of public meetings for need analysis. For example McKillip (1987) gives suggested rules of procedure for *Public Hearings* where members of a committee hear evidence from witnesses, raise questions, cross-examine them and issue a report (see also Mater, 1984). A less formalized version is the *Community Meeting.* Typically this is an evening meeting where concerned members of the community involved address the issues as they see them. Again it is possible to give suggestions likely to increase the effectiveness of such meetings, including wide prior advertizing and procedural rules enforced by a firm chair. Such events can raise issues for consideration, and also the consciousness of the community involved.

```
1) Group Techniques, including:
   a.  Focus Groups and
   b.  Public Meetings.
2) Surveys, including:
   a.  Client Surveys and
   b.  Key Informant Surveys.
3) Interviews, including:
   a.  Client Interviews and
   b.  Key Informant Interviews.
4) Analysis of Existing Data.
```

Figure A.2 *Methods for assessing needs*

This latter can be something of a double-edged sword. Increase in awareness of, and of subsequent participation in, a program or project is a valuable spinoff. However, the raising of false hopes of the introduction of a program which subsequently does not materialize is not unknown. Nor the raising of false fears about the dangers of, say, a community facility for persons with psychological disorders.

Surveys. As in many other fields of evaluation and applied social research, surveys are widely used in needs analysis. Both self-completion or interview-based versions are possible. The general relative advantages and disadvantages of the two formats are as discussed in Chapter 5, which also covers some of the practicalities of mounting a worthwhile survey.

The quickest and cheapest version is probably the *Key Informant Survey*. Key informants are persons or representatives who are in a position to have an informed knowledge and understanding of the likely needs of those for whom the program or service is planned. Service providers including officers and field workers, community representatives both formal (e.g. local councillors) and voluntary (e.g. leaders of groups and associations), other professionals (e.g. doctors and other health specialists, police and legal specialists, teachers and advisory service representatives) are some possibilities – depending on the type of program proposed.

There are likely to be major problems in securing representativeness in these informants. Local knowledge and networking in the community should help you to avoid those likely to give a distorted or idiosyncratic perception of needs. Because key informants are, by virtue of their positions, likely to have substantial influence on the successful running of the program taking serious note of their views is, in itself, likely to have a beneficial effect.

However, it is highly likely that assessment of need will vary between informants and conflicts may have to be resolved. Even in the unlikely event of consensus, funding shortfall and other practicalities may lead to disappointment with the outcome and possible counter-productive effects of the whole exercise.

Consumer or *Client Surveys* are common and have the obvious and important advantage of giving a voice to those to whom the program or service is addressed. The most meticulously planned service is of no value if clients don't use it. Or rather it is of negative value as it is taking up resources which otherwise might be made available elsewhere. So, addressing perceived needs of potential clients by one means or another is an essential, and surveys provide a relatively cost-effective way of doing this. Figure A.3 covers some of the issues involved. Figure A.4 lists some of the problems likely to be encountered when conducting client surveys and suggests some possible solutions. Some groups are difficult to reach through survey techniques. Even with such groups there are possibilities. For example, Hallberg (1998) discusses approaches to assessing the needs of elderly persons with communication difficulties, and Repper and Perkins (1998) those of people with serious mental health problems.

Interviews. Surveys, composed essentially of closed questions (i.e. calling for 'yes/no' or other answers with a number of prespecified possible alternatives), can be administered in an interview situation (either face to face or by telephone). This closed nature tends to fit in best with a situation where it is felt that much of the needs can be prespecified and

---

1) *Design of the survey questionnaire is driven by the needs you require information about.* Go for those aspects you can't reach by other means (e.g. from existing records, interviews, or observation) or where you wish to cross-check on other sources of information.

2) *The general rules about questionnaire design apply.* A good questionnaire has to be carefully crafted to avoid leading, confusing and ambiguous questions. Seek specialist assistance if you do not have the necessary skills.

3) *You are concerned with obtaining informed opinions based on respondents' direct experience or knowledge.* For example facts about themselves and others about which they have direct knowledge such as family members. Questions have to be targeted so they access such information.

4) *Avoid asking global questions about the adequacy of services, requests for direct statements of needs or lists of solutions.* You are likely to get contradictory answers and to raise unrealistic expectations.

5) *A needs assessment questionnaire is NOT a public opinion poll.* The latter usually calls for global judgements about education, health services, crime, etc., heavily influenced by media exposure and not necessarily grounded in personal experience.

6) *Questionnaires can be targeted at different populations.* This will usually be the potential users of a projected service or program, but could also be potential service or program providers. The content will need to be tailored appropriately.

7) *Avoid distribution methods likely to result in low response rates and/or a self-selected sample.* For example while it may be tempting to take up an offer of publication in a local newspaper or community newsletter this type of distribution is likely to result in both these problems leading to data of very dubious representativeness. Mail surveys should only be used if resources permit the inclusion of a stamped addressed envelope, and a follow-up mailing to non-respondents.

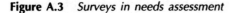

Figure A.3   *Surveys in needs assessment*

Difficulties	Possible solutions
• Clients may not be able to make valid comments about proposed programs	• Provides a challenge for you to present issues in an accessible and meaningful way
• Clients may not appreciate the range of alternatives	• Spell them out
• Clients only interested in short term	• Short-term experiences and effects may be important to successful functioning of program
• Client ratings are invariably positive	• Applies mainly to ongoing programs. Can ask directly for critical comments
• The clients responding may not be representative	• Important to get high response rate to reduce possibility of sampling bias
• Clients only tell you what they think you want to hear	• Not to the needs they have relating to proposed programs/services

Figure A.4   *Perceived difficulties with client surveys – and possible solutions*

the task is more to establish quantitative information about who, where, and how many. More open-ended interviews provide a good opportunity for discovering people's needs as they themselves perceive them. Or for using key informants to give the developers ideas and suggestions for how the needs are best conceptualized and specified.

Such semi-structured or depth interviews (see Chapter 5) are time-consuming both in their actual administration and, particularly, in their subsequent analysis. They also require greater personal and professional skills on the part of the interviewer if good quality data are to be obtained. Nevertheless they provide a very worthwhile investment of resources to complement other approaches and can help both in understanding the nature of the needs and communicating them (for example by the use of vivid quotations).

Analysis of Existing Data

It is almost certain there will already be in existence sources of data relevant to your needs analysis. There are pitfalls in using data for one purpose that have already been collected for a different purpose, as discussed in Chapter 5. Data collected for purposes other than research where there may not have been a concern for reliability and validity must be treated cautiously. For example, data compiled by a professional group on the amount of unpaid over-time they put in as part of a salary claim may suffer from over-estimation, whilst the under-recording of hours attributable to accidents at work submitted by employers to a regulating body is not beyond the bounds of possibility. Even data not likely to suffer from obvious bias are likely to have to be 'translated' in one way or another. Estimates have to be made about the effects of differences of time, place and population between the setting in which the data are collected and that to which they are to be applied. Hence, here as elsewhere, such data should not be used as the only source of information.

Reports. Existing programs or services in your own locality and elsewhere can be a major source of information about the nature of the program and those who use it. Reports and returns for monitoring and evaluation purposes differ widely in the quality and quantity of what is included. Existing needs analyses themselves may be very useful. There is a strong tendency for program developers to seek to reinvent the wheel with each new program. Any gains in time and trouble to be made from adopting and adapting what others have done before should be seized with alacrity.

In practice, of course, you are unlikely to be carrying out a needs analysis for a program equivalent to one already running in your area – although stranger things have happened. So the 'translation' issue mentioned above is relevant. Subjective judgements about the similarity, and hence applicability, to your situation have to be made. But even if there is little you can use directly, ideas about the approach to the task (possibly by seeing the disadvantages of the one taken previously) might develop.

Data Archives. In similar vein, local agency-based information about users of existing services (who they are and where they come from, both geographically and in terms of referral) may be available and usable.

National and regional level sources are also available. Most developed countries now have a range of information relevant to needs analysis in publications and data archives which can be accessed in print form, CD-ROM and increasingly via the World Wide Web. Such archive data can be used to describe the target population for the program or service covering characteristics such as age, income, gender, ethnic background and place of residence. In the UK the 'Index of Local Conditions' developed by the Department of the Environment provides a measure of relative levels of deprivation across areas of England based on a set of indicators such as unemployment, overcrowding and educational participation. Porteous (1996) gives details and discusses a number of local case studies using this approach to provide local measures of social need and deprivation.

The ready availability of geographical information systems (GIS) software now makes it feasible to display directly the geographic location of the target population on a map of appropriate scale.

McKillip (1998, pp 267–8) gives a set of US sources for these data archives and also describes techniques of 'synthetic estimation' which allow estimates of the target population and its characteristics to be estimated from data available for a population different from the target population.

1) Use information on needs from prior needs analysis carried out in developing program. If no prior needs analysis then, if feasible, carry out 'mini' needs analysis at this stage.
2) Assess the extent to which target audience are program clients. Likely use of survey/questionnaire techniques with program clients (may be combined with other data-gathering exercises).
3) Assess whether program meets needs of clients involved using:
   • methods as in Figure A.2 with clients;
   • observation of process; and
   • measurement of outcomes (including achievement of goals and objectives where appropriate).

Figure A.5   *Assessing needs in current programs*

Putting It Together

There has been a tendency for needs analysis to be viewed either as a 'top-down' or 'bottom-up' task. The former emphasizes the views and concerns of key informants, particularly service providers and 'experts', and values the kind of 'objective' data provided by analysing quantitative information whether pre-existing or survey derived. The latter regards the subjective views of potential clients or consumers as central.

The scale and complexity of your needs analysis obviously depend crucially on the time and other resources available. Its nature will be influenced by your own priorities as well as the concerns of those to whom you report. As emphasized above, total reliance on existing data is dangerous because of its having been collected for other purposes. Also it is unlikely to lead to a fundamental review of the problem, if only because it is necessarily derived from 'what is'. Concentrating solely on the views of the client is similarly problematic, because of the likely methodological deficiencies in client surveys or group meetings, and the heavy resource implications of reliance on interviewing. A mix of methods seems indicated, drawing upon both existing and new data, and using both quantitative and qualitative methods.

These general issues apply whatever the particular field of the needs analysis. Browne (1996) and Baldwin (1998) cover specific issues in needs assessment in relation to community care. Case studies of particular community care needs are given in Black (1998) (rehabilitation services); Repper and Perkins (1998) (severe mental health problems); and Hallberg (1998) (elderly people with communication difficulties and/or cognitive impairment). See also discussions relating to health needs (Foreman, 1996); community needs (Percy-Smith, 1996); housing needs (Hawtin, 1996); needs for legal services (Blake, 1996); and labour market and training needs (Campbell, 1996).

Whatever mix of methods you come up with, the 'steps in need analysis' (Figure A.1) provides a useful aide-mémoire of the aspects to keep in mind. If you are an insider, or otherwise have local knowledge, your experience and informal understandings and insights into the situation should not be ignored in providing a context and (tentatively) filling in any gaps left by your data collection. Finally, remember that without a report which communicates effectively to those who are to use the needs analysis, the whole thing will have been a waste of time!

Note. When assessing whether or not a program or service CURRENTLY RUNNING is meeting the needs of the target population, essentially the same methods and techniques can be used as those covered in needs analysis for a proposed program – see Figure A.5.

APPENDIX B: EFFICIENCY (COST AND BENEFIT) ANALYSIS

It seems eminently reasonable that some form of assessment of the relative costs and benefits of a service or program should play a major part in decisions about its continuation, expansion or even closure. Many evaluations present much information about outcomes, from which benefits (or, perhaps, lack of benefits) could be deduced. Relatively few mention costs. This may be because it is not an easy task to quantify the cost of a program. Or because it is regarded more as the province of the auditor or finance department than of the evaluator. However, while some procedures used in cost-benefit and cost-effectiveness analyses (the most common forms of efficiency analyses) are highly technical this does not justify omission of information directly relevant to many evaluations. Simply thinking in terms of the costs or efforts involved in setting up and running a program, perhaps in relation to other possible programs, can help in developing a more structured and principled analysis than the impressionistic 'evaluation' decision-makers are prone to use.

Costs

Costs are the various inputs, both direct and indirect, required to set up and run a program or mount an intervention. They are the time, space, facilities, equipment, supplies, staff and other resources needed, without which it wouldn't happen. Even when the space is already available, the physical resources are donated, and the staff are volunteers the program still represents an *Opportunity Cost*. In other words, because the resources are being expended in this way, other opportunities are forgone.

Relative costing. When the main evaluative concern is to compare two programs, or two variants of a program, it is sometimes possible to make reasonable assumptions that one is more resource intensive. In other words it costs more than the other. For example, an intervention program run by parents may be assumed to be cheaper than one run by professionals. If the outcomes of the two do not differ, this suggests the parent-run program is preferable.

However, such assumptions require careful analysis. Yates (1998) considers problems with the common assumption that outpatient care is far less expensive than the cost of inpatient care. For example, families who play a part in that care typically have curtailed opportunities for employment, in addition to restrictions on their private and social life, which should be entered into the equation. He cites McGuire (1991), who found the care of schizophrenics at home required almost twice the resources as care in a public facility. This is when both monetary outlays are taken into consideration as well as the time devoted by the family to activities related to the treatment.

Cost-Effectiveness and Cost-Benefit Analyses

Traditional *Cost-Effectiveness Analysis* compares costs measured in monetary terms (pounds, dollars, euros, etc.) with outcomes measured in whatever unit appears most sensible. Thus a traffic-calming scheme might be rated as costing £2,000 for each road accident involving personal injury reduced. Outcomes can be multiple and some form of index may need to be developed. For example, fatal accidents are, say, given a weighting of 10; accidents involving hospitalization weighted 2; and other reported accidents given single weighting. Typically, comparisons are made between different schemes or programs using the same basis for assessing outcomes.

In *Cost-Benefit Analysis* both costs and outcomes are measured in the same unit, usually monetary. Dividing the costs expended by the benefits which accrue gives the *Benefit-Cost Ratio*. A ratio greater than one indicates the program produces greater value than it consumes. Other things being equal, a program with a higher benefit-cost ratio is preferable to one with a lower ratio.

While these analyses are conceptually straightforward, the devil is, as ever, in the detail. The main problems are, first, deciding what to include, both for costs and for outcomes. And, secondly, how to operationalize them so as to reach summary figures.

Measuring Costs

Several disciplines, notably economics, have wrestled with the problem of measuring costs. The traditional economists' definition in terms of how much a consumer is prepared to pay for goods or services is of limited use in many public service programs. Programs may be provided without charge, or at less than the full cost. Their clients are seldom in a position to 'shop around' in deciding which of a number of possible alternative programs to choose.

A conceptually simple approach is to measure what actually is spent. In the evaluation of a new program, this calls for consideration of costs at a very early stage of the process, if development costs are to be included in the equation. If such costs are to be ignored and consideration limited to the costs involved in running the program, then the means of measuring costs can be built in to the design stage of the project. In the not uncommon situation where evaluation is called for at a relatively late stage, even the measurement of actual running costs may not be feasible and some form of estimation may have to be used.

People and Time

For virtually all social programs, by far the most important cost is the time of those involved in running it. Program personnel of various types, including professionals, assistants, managers, administrative and secretarial support, cleaners, drivers, etc., spend time. The time of clients themselves is an integral part of programs.

A proper assessment of cost calls for a measurement of the time spent by each agent with each client in each of the various activities and procedures which make up the program. These times are then multiplied by the value of that particular person's time, e.g. an appropriate fraction of their salary. Yates (1996, pp. 28-41) gives detailed suggestions of several ways in which this may be done, and of paper and spreadsheet (and other computer) approaches to capturing the data. For administrative and other support staff who do not have direct dealings with individual clients, proportionate costs attributable to individuals can be calculated, based on the number of clients and the extent to which the centre has other responsibilities as well as the program. The value of the time spent by the clients themselves is often regarded as nil. In some circumstances this appears unreasonable, particularly for those who have to forgo paid employment or have to ask others to take over their responsibilities to take part.

More generally, there may be substantial costs incurred by the family, partners or friends of the client. The parent of a child with disabilities or other special needs working at home on some kind of structured program may devote many hours to this which are a central part both of the program and its costs. It is of course possible a successful program will also contribute to the benefits side of the ledger. Improvements in functioning may lead to a subsequent reduced call for parental support and less use of expensive specialized facilities.

While a detailed cost assessment may be feasible for some small-scale evaluations when correspondingly small numbers of personnel are involved, it may in itself be viewed as adding unacceptable additional bureaucracy and costs. Sampling and estimation can reduce the resources needed. This can provide worthwhile data providing likely biases are anticipated and efforts made to nullify them. Asking workers retrospectively to detail the time they spent on various activities with clients may lead to over- or underestimates depending on how the task is viewed. Combining this with at-the-time sampled filling-in of logs, or of direct observation, would increase the dependability of the data. Figure B.1 gives an example of such a log (see also Yates, 1996).

As previously discussed and agreed with meetings of staff representatives we are conducting a survey of administrative, teaching, pastoral and research activities. This is so we can provide an accurate estimate of the costs of professional staff input.

This information will be only available to the evaluators responsible for cost assessment who are independent consultants. Data will only be used for the purposes of this survey, the results of which will be published in an anonymized format. Many thanks for your time in completing this log.

Week starting / / (Monday to Sunday inclusive).

Please include ALL work-related activity actually carried out during the week. Enter total number of minutes per day and overall week total

Activity	Mon	Tues	Wed	Thurs	Fri	Sat	Sun	Week total
Direct teaching								
Pastoral								
Admin (meetings)								
Admin (other)								
Research								
Teaching related								
Other 1 (specify):								
Other 2 (specify):								
Other 3 (specify):								

Note: Full definitions of the various activities should be provided.

Figure B.1   *Time allocation log*

Facilities and other Physical Resources

The facilities needed to run a program obviously vary greatly between programs. Some require specialized clinics or other premises which may be very expensive to run, and which make up a large proportion of costs. Others take place in the clients' homes or in community facilities where no direct charge is made and even the coffee and biscuits are freely given. Nevertheless all such facilities are a part of what is needed to run the program and a realistic evaluation should seek to apportion their cost.

The same basic approach to that used with personnel can be taken in costing physical accommodation. A global figure for these costs over the duration under consideration may be acceptable. If attempts are to be made to distribute costs at the level of individual clients then it will be necessary to consider the total number of clients and the amount of time each is involved with the program. Lease, rent or depreciation costs can be used to assess the value of the resources used. Yates (1996, pp. 41-4) gives details.

Other physical resources likely to be involved include:

• *Equipment* – specialized equipment is central to some programs; all are likely to call for computers, telephones, copiers, fax machines, desks, chairs, etc. Costing is typically based on depreciation of market value, appropriately proportionalized. Costs of use of the equipment, including email, Internet, etc., should be taken into account.

- *Consumables* – anything given to the client which is non-returnable. Purchase cost of the item (or of its equivalent if the item itself were donated).
- *Supplies* – paper, computer disks, coffee, etc. Purchase cost.
- *Financing and insurance* – if the program or service has required external financing, including where it runs as a result of funding from government sources or a charitable foundation, this should obviously be included. Also the premium of any insurance needed to protect those involved from excessive financial costs in the event of fire or theft, professional liability, injury, etc.
- *Transport* – for some programs, the transport of clients to a central facility can be a major cost. Similarly some call for program staff to deliver the program on an outreach basis. If standard rates are not available, total vehicle expenses attributable to the program will have to be computed.

Other Perspectives on Costs

The costs of a program are likely to be viewed differently by different interest groups. The case for an evaluation to be responsive to these different constituencies was made in Chapter 2. Taking account of these other perspectives when seeking to assess the costs of a program may well guard against the omission of important costs.

APPENDIX C: CODE OF ETHICS

Utility

The utility standards are intended to ensure that an evaluation will serve the information needs of intended users.

U1 *Stakeholder Identification* Persons involved in or affected by the evaluation should be identified so that their needs can be addressed.

U2 *Evaluator Credibility* The persons conducting the evaluation should be both trustworthy and competent to perform the evaluation so that the evaluation findings achieve maximum credibility and acceptance.

U3 *Information Scope and Selection* Information collected should be broadly selected to address pertinent questions about the program and be responsive to the needs and interests of clients and other specified stakeholders.

U4 *Values Identification* The perspectives, procedures, and rationale used to interpret the findings should be carefully described so that the bases for value judgments are clear.

U5 *Report Clarity* Evaluation reports should clearly describe the program being evaluated, including its context, and the purposes, procedures, and findings of the evaluation so that essential information is provided and easily understood.

U6 *Report Timeliness and Dissemination* Significant interim findings and evaluation reports should be disseminated to intended users so that they can be used in a timely fashion.

U7 *Evaluation Impact* Evaluations should be planned, conducted, and reported in ways that encourage follow-through by stakeholders so that the likelihood that the evaluation will be used is increased.

Feasibility

The feasibility standards are intended to ensure that an evaluation will be realistic, prudent, diplomatic, and frugal.

F1 *Practical Procedures* The evaluation procedures should be practical to keep disruption to a minimum while needed information is obtained.

F2 *Political Viability* The evaluation should be planned and conducted with anticipation of the different positions of various interest groups so that their cooperation may be obtained and so that possible attempts by any of these groups to curtail evaluation operations or to bias or misapply the results can be averted or counteracted.

F3	*Cost-Effectiveness*	The evaluation should be efficient and produce information of sufficient value so that the resources expended can be justified.

Propriety

The propriety standards are intended to ensure that an evaluation will be conducted legally, ethically, and with due regard for the welfare of those involved in the evaluation, as well as those affected by its results.

P1	*Service Orientation*	Evaluations should be designed to assist organizations to address and effectively serve the needs of the full range of targeted participants.

P2	*Formal Agreements*	Obligations of the formal parties to an evaluation (what is to be done, how, by whom, when) should be agreed to in writing so that these parties are obligated to adhere to all conditions of the agreement or formally to renegotiate it.

P3	*Rights of Human Subjects*	Evaluations should be designed and conducted to respect and protect the rights and welfare of human subjects.

P4	*Human Interactions*	Evaluators should respect human dignity and worth in their interactions with other persons associated with an evaluation so that participants are not threatened or harmed.

P5	*Complete and Fair Assessment*	The evaluation should be complete and fair in its examination and recording of strengths and weaknesses of the program being evaluated so that strengths can be built upon and problem areas addressed.

P6	*Disclosure of Findings*	The formal parties to an evaluator should ensure that the full set of evaluation findings along with pertinent limitations are made accessible to the persons affected by the evaluation and any others with expressed legal rights to receive the results.

P7	*Conflict of Interest*	Conflict of interest should be dealt with openly and honestly, so that it does not compromise the evaluation processes and results.

P8	*Fiscal Responsibility*	The evaluator's allocation and expenditure of resources should reflect sound accountability procedures and otherwise be prudent and ethically responsible so that expenditures are accounted for and appropriate.

Accuracy

The accuracy standards are intended to ensure that an evaluation will reveal and convey technically adequate information about the features that determine worth of merit of the program being evaluated.

A1 *Program Documentation* The program being evaluated should be described and documented clearly and accurately so that the program is clearly identified.

A2 *Context Analysis* The context in which the program exists should be examined in enough detail so that its likely influences on the program can be identified.

A3 *Described Purposes and Procedures* The purposes and procedures of the evaluation should be monitored and described in enough detail so that they can be identified and assessed.

A4 *Defensible Information Sources* The sources of information used in a program evaluation should be described in enough detail so that the adequacy of the information can be assessed.

A5 *Valid Information* The information-gathering procedures should be chosen or developed and then implemented so that they will ensure that the interpretation arrived at is valid for the intended use.

A6 *Reliable Information* The information-gathering procedures should be chosen or developed and then implemented so that they will ensure that the information obtained is sufficiently reliable for the intended use.

A7 *Systematic Information* The information collected, processed, and reported in an evaluation should be systematically reviewed and any errors found should be corrected.

A8 *Analysis of Quantitative Information* Quantitative information in an evaluation should be appropriately and systematically analyzed so that evaluation questions are effectively answered.

A9 *Analysis of Qualitative Information* Qualitative information in an evaluation should be appropriately and systematically analyzed so that evaluation questions are effectively answered.

A10 *Justified Conclusions* The conclusions reached in an evaluation should be explicitly justified so that stakeholders can assess them.

A11 *Impartial Reporting* Reporting procedures should guard against distortion caused by personal feelings and biases of any party to the evaluation so that evaluation reports fairly reflect the evaluation findings.

A12 *Meta-evaluation* The evaluation itself should be formatively and summatively evaluated against these and other pertinent standards so that its conduct is appropriately guided and, on completion, stakeholders can closely examine its strengths and weaknesses.

Source: Joint Committee on Standards (1994) *Program evaluation standards.* 2nd edn. Sage Publications, Inc. Reprinted with permission.

REFERENCES AND AUTHOR INDEX

The references incorporate an author index. The numbers in bold at the end of each entry indicate the page(s) where the publication is referred to in this book.

Adler, P. A. and Adler, P. (1987) *Membership Roles in Field Research*. Newbury Park, Calif: Sage. **96**

Alderson, P. (1996) Ethics and research directed towards effective outcomes. In A. Oakley and H. Roberts (eds.) *Evaluating Social Interventions: A Report of Two Workshops Funded by the Economic and Social Research Council*. Ilford: Barnardo's. **33, 40**

American Evaluation Association (1995) Guiding principles for evaluators. In W. R. Shadish, D. L. Newman, M. A. Scheirer and C. Wye (eds.) *New Directions for Program Evaluation*. No. 66. San Francisco: Jossey-Bass. **29**.

Anastasi, A. (1988) *Psychological Testing*. 6th Edn. New York: Macmillan. **99**.

Atkinson, P. and Delamont, S. (1985) Bread and Dreams or Bread and Circuses? a critique of 'case study' research in education. In M. Shipman (ed.) *Educational Research, Principles, Policies and Practices*. London: Falmer. **21**.

Baldwin, S. (ed.) (1998) *Needs Assessment and Community Care: Clinical Practice and Policy Making*. Oxford: Butterworth-Heinemann. **127, 134**.

Barkdoll, G. L. (1980) Type III evaluations: consultation and consensus. *Public Administration Review*, 40, 174–79. **15**.

Becker, H. S. (1998) *Tricks of the Trade: How to Think about your Research while you're Doing it*. Chicago: University of Chicago Press. **53**.

Berk, R. A. and Rossi, P. H. (1990) *Thinking about Program Evaluation*. Newbury Park, Calif: Sage. **128**.

Bhaskar, R. (1978) *A Realist Theory of Science*. Brighton: Harvester Press. **71**.

Bhaskar, R. (1986) *Scientific Realism and Human Emancipation*. London: Verso. **71**.

Bickman, L. and Rog, D. J. (eds.) (1998) *Handbook of Applied Social Research Methods*. Thousand Oaks, Calif: Sage. **82**.

Bickman, L. and Salzer, M. S. (1997) Introduction: Measuring quality in mental health services. *Evaluation Review*, 21, 285–91. **64**.

Black, K. (1998) Needs assessment in a rehabilitation service. In S. Baldwin (ed.). *Needs Assessment and Community Care: Clinical Practice and Policy Making*. Oxford: Butterworth Heinnemann. **134**.

Blaikie, N. (1993) *Approaches to Social Enquiry*. Cambridge: Polity Press. **71**.

Blake, A. (1996) Assessing needs for legal services. In J. Percy-Smith (ed.). *Needs Assessment in Public Policy*. Milton Keynes: Open University Press. **134**.

Bramel, D. and Friend, R. (1981) Hawthorne, the myth of the docile worker, and class bias in psychology. *American Psychologist*, 36, 867–78. **38**.

British Association of Social Workers (1996) *The Code of Ethics for Social Work*. Birmingham: BASW. **28**.

British Sociological Association (1989a) *BSA Guidelines on Anti-Sexist Language*. London: BSA (mimeo). **124**.

British Sociological Association (1989b) *BSA Guidelines on Anti-Racist Language*. London: BSA (mimeo). **124**.

Browne, M. (1996) Needs assessment and community care. In J. Percy-Smith (ed.). Needs Assessment in Public Policy. Milton Keynes: Open University Press. **134**.

Bryman, A. and Cramer, D. (1997) *Quantitative Data Analysis with SPSS for Windows: A Guide for Social Scientists.* London: Routledge. **114**.

Cairncross, S., Carruthers, I., Curtis, D., Feachem, R., Bradley, D. and Baldwin, G. (1980) *Evaluation for Village Water Supply Planning.* Chichester: Wiley. **10**.

Campbell, D. T. (1969) Reforms as experiments. *American Psychologist*, 24, 409–29. **41, 124**.

Campbell, D. T. and Stanley, J. C. (1966) *Experimental and Quasi-Experimental Designs for Research.* Chicago: Rand McNally. **11, 58**.

Campbell, M. (1996) Assessing labour market and training needs. In J. Percy-Smith (ed.). Needs Assessment in Public Policy. Milton Keynes. Open University Press. **134**.

Cheetham, J., Fuller, R., McIvor, G. and Petch, A. (1992) *Evaluating Social Work Effectiveness.* Milton Keynes: Open University Press. **28**.

Chen, H.-T. (1990) *Theory Driven Evaluations.* Newbury Park, Calif: Sage. **51, 69, 70**.

Coffey, A. and Atkinson, P. (1996) *Making Sense of Qualitative Data: Complementary Research Strategies.* Thousand Oaks, Calif: Sage. **118**.

Cook, T. D. and Campbell, D. T. (1979) *Quasi-Experimentation: Design and Analysis Issues for Field Settings.* Chicago: Rand McNally. **58**.

Cook, T. D. and Devine, E. C. (1982) Trying to discover explanatory processes through meta-analysis. Paper presented at the National Meeting of the American Educational Research Association, March, New York. **72**.

Cousins, J. B. and Earl, L. M. (1992) The case for participatory evaluation. *Educational Evaluation and Policy Analysis*, 14, 397–418. **19**.

Cousins, J. B. and Earl, L. M. (eds.) (1995) *Participatory Evaluation in Education: Studies in Evaluation Use and Organisational Learning.* London: Falmer. **19, 24, 25, 26**.

Cronbach, L. J. (1963) Course improvement through evaluation. *Teachers College Record*, 64, 672–83. **11**.

Cronbach, L. J. (1982) *Designing Evaluations of Educational and Social Programs.* San Francisco: Jossey-Bass. **51, 126**.

Denzin, N. K. (1988) *The Research Act: A Theoretical Introduction to Sociological Methods.* 3rd Edn. Englewood Cliffs, NJ: Prentice-Hall. **97**.

Duguid, S. and Pawson, R. (1998) Education, change and transformation: the prison experience. *Evaluation Review*, 22, 470–95. **74**.

Earl, L. M. and Cousins, J. B. (1995) *Classroom Assessment: Changing the Face; Facing the Change.* Toronto: Ontario Public School Teacher Federation. **25**.

Elliott, J. (1991) *Action Research for Educational Change.* Milton Keynes: Open University Press. **21**.

ERS Standards Committee (1982) Evaluation Research Society standards for program Evaluation. In P. H. Rossi (ed.) *Standards for Program Evaluation (New Directions for Program Evaluation no. 15).* San Francisco: Jossey-Bass. **29**.

Everitt, A. and Hardiker, P. (1996) *Evaluating for Good Practice.* London: Macmillan. **22**.

Fetterman, D. M. (1989) *Ethnography: Step by Step.* Newbury Park, Calif: Sage. **96**.

Fetterman, D. M. (1998) Ethnography. In L. Bickman and D.J. Rog (eds.). Handbook of Applied Social Research Methods. Thousand Oaks, Calif: Sage. **96.**.

Fink, A. (1995) *Evaluation for Education and Psychology.* Thousand Oaks, Calif: Sage. **11, 23**.

Foreman, A. (1996) Health needs assessment. In J. Percy-Smith (ed.). Needs Assessment in Public Policy. Milton Keynes: Open University Press. **134**.

Foster, J. J. (1998) *Data Analysis using SPSS for Windows: A Beginner's Guide.* London: Sage. **114**.

Fowler, F. J. (1998) Design and evaluation of survey questions. In L. Bickman and D. J. Rog (eds.). Handbook of Applied Social Research Methods. Thousand Oaks, Calif: Sage. **84, 85**.

Gahan, C. and Hannibal, M. (1998) *Doing Qualitative Research Using QSR NUD.IST.* London: Sage. **119**.

Glaser, B. and Strauss, A. I. (1967) *The Discovery of Grounded Theory.* Chicago: Aldine. **119**.

Gorman, D. M. (1998) The irrelevance of evidence in the development of school-based drug prevention policy, 1986–1996. *Evaluation Review*, 22, 118–46. **55**.

Grady, K. E. and Wallston, B. S. (1988) *Research in Health Care Settings*. Newbury Park, Calif: Sage. **79**.

Greene, J. C. (1994) Qualitative program evaluation: practice and promise. In N. K.Denzin and Y. S. Lincoln (eds.) *Handbook of Qualitative Research*. Thousand Oaks, Calif: Sage. **10**.

Guba, E. G. and Lincoln, Y. S. (1989) *Fourth Generation Evaluation*. Newbury Park, Calif: Sage. **11, 127**.

Hakim, C. (1987) *Research Design: Strategies and Choices in the Design of Social Research*. London: Allen & Unwin. **45**.

Hallberg, I. R. (1998) Needs assessment in elderly people suffering from communication difficulties and/or cognitive impairment. In S. Baldwin (ed.). Needs Assessment and Community Care: Clinical Practice and Policy Making. Oxford: Butterworth-Heinemann. **13, 134**.

Harré, R. (1972) *The Philosophies of Science*. Oxford: Oxford University Press. **71**.

Hawtin, M. (1996) Assessing housing needs. In J. Percy-Smith (ed.). Needs Assessment in Public Policy, Milton Keynes: Open University Press. **134**.

Henry, G. (1997) Creating effective graphs: solutions for a variety of evaluation data. *New Directions for Evaluation no. 73*. San Francisco: Jossey-Bass. **115, 121**.

Herman, J. L., Morris, L. L. and Fitz-Gibbon, C. T. (1987) *Evaluator's Handbook*. Thousand Oaks, Calif: Sage. **52**.

Hodder, I. (1994) The interpretation of documents and material culture. In N. K. Denzin and Y. S. Lincoln (eds.) *The Handbook of Qualitative Research*. Thousand Oaks, Calif: Sage. **101**.

House, E. R. (1991) Realism in research. *Educational Researcher*, 20, 2–9. **71**.

Huberman, M. (1990) Linkage between researchers and practitioners: a qualitative study. *American Educational Research Journal*, 27, 363–91. **19**.

Huberman, M. (1995) The many modes of participatory evaluation. In J.B. Cousins and L.M. Earl (eds.). Participatory Evaluation in Education: Studies in Evaluation Use and Organisational Learning. London: Falmer. **19, 22**.

James, M. (1993) Evaluation for policy: rationality and political reality: the paradigm case of PRAISE? In R. G. Burgess (ed.) *Educational Research and Evaluation: For Policy and Practice?* London: Falmer. **42**.

Johnson, S. (1997) Continuity and change: a study of how women cope with the transition to professional programmes of higher education. University of Huddersfield, PhD thesis. **88, 91**.

Joint Committee on Standards (1994) *Program Evaluation Standards*. 2nd Edn. Thousand Oaks, Calif: Sage. **29, 141**.

Jones, E. M., Gottfredson, G. D. and Gottfredson, D. C. (1997) Success for some: an evaluation of a success for all program. *Evaluation Review*, 21, 643–70. **55**.

Judd, C. M. and Kenny, D. A. (1981) Process analysis: estimating mediation in treatment evaluations. *Evaluation Review*, 5, 602–19. **51**.

Kazi, M. A. F. (1998a) *Single-Case Evaluation by Social Workers*. Aldershot: Ashgate. **60**.

Kazi, M.A.F. (1998b) Scientific Realist Evaluation of Social Work Practice. Paper presented at the European Evaluation Society Conference, October, Rome. **74**.

King, J. A. (1995) Involving practitioners in evaluation studies: how viable is collaborative evaluation in schools? In J.B. Cousins and L.M. Earl (eds.). Participatory Evaluation in Education: Studies in Evaluation Use and Organisational Learning. London: Falmer. **19, 20, 21**.

Kline, P. (1986) *A Handbook of Test Construction*. London: Methuen. **99**.

Kline, P. (1993) *The Handbook of Psychological Testing*. London: Routledge. **99**.

Klockars, C. B. (1974) *The Professional Fence*. Glencoe, Ill: Free Press. **34**.

Lavrakas, P. J. (1998) Methods for sampling and interviewing in telephone surveys. In L. Bickman and D. J. Rog (eds.). *Handbook of Applied Social Research Methods*. Thousand Oaks, Calif: Sage. **89**.

Lewin, K. (1951) Problems of research in social psychology. In D. Cartwright (ed.) *Field Theory in Social Science*. New York: Harper & Brothers. **69**.

Loewenthal, M. (1996) *An Introduction to Psychological Tests and Scales*. London: UCL Press. **99**.

MacDonald, B. (1976) Evaluation and the control of education. In D. Tawney (ed.), *Curriculum Evaluation Today: Trends and Implications*. London: Macmillan. **67**

Mangione, T. W. (1998) Mail surveys. In L. Bickman and D. Rog (eds.). *Handbook of Applied Social Research Methods*. Thousand Oaks: Sage. **84**.

Martin, J. (1981) A garbage can model of the psychological research process. *American Behavioral Scientist*, 25, 131–151. **79**.

Mater, J. (1984) *Public Hearings, Procedures and Strategies*. Englewood Cliffs, NJ: Prentice-Hall. **129**.

McCord, J. (1978) A thirty year follow-up of treatment effects. *American Psychologist*, 33, 284–91. **38**.

McGuire, T. G. (1991) Measuring the economic costs of schizophrenia. *Schizophrenia Bulletin*, 17, 375–94. **137**.

McKillip, J. (1987) *Need Analysis: Tools for the Human Services and Education*. Newbury Park, Calif: Sage. **127, 129**.

McKillip, J. (1998) *Need analysis: process and techniques*. In L. Bickman and D. J. Rog (eds.). *Handbook of Applied Social Research Methods*. Thousand Oaks, Calif: Sage. **127, 129, 133**.

McTaggart, R. (1991) *A Brief History of Action Research*. Geelong, Victoria: Deaking University Press. **21**.

Mertens, D. M. (1998) *Research Methods in Education and Psychology: Integrating Diversity with Quantitative and Qualitative Approaches*. Thousand Oaks, Calif: Sage. **98**.

Miles, M. B. and Huberman, A. M. (1994) *Qualitative Data Analysis: An Expanded Sourcebook*. 2nd Edn. Thousand Oaks, Calif: Sage. **103**.

Milgram, S. (1963) Behavioral study of obedience. *Journal of Abnormal and Social Psychology*, 67, 371–8. **32**.

Mohr, L. B. (1995) *Impact Analysis for Program Evaluation*. 2nd Edn. Thousand Oaks, Calif: Sage. **43, 51, 61**.

Nerdrum, P. (1997) Maintenance of the effect of training in communication skills: a controlled follow-up study of level of communicated empathy. *British Journal of Social Work*, 27, 705–22. **62**.

Newman, D. L. and Brown, R. D. (1996) *Applied Ethics for Program Evaluation*. Thousand Oaks, Calif: Sage. **29**.

Oakley, A. and Fullerton, D. (1996) The lamp-post of research: support or illumination? In A. Oakley and H. Roberts (eds.) *Evaluating Social Interventions*. Ilford: Barnardo's. **57**.

Parsons, H. M. (1974) What happened at Hawthorne? *Science*, 183, 922–31. **38**.

Patton, M. Q. (1978) *Utilisation-Focused Evaluation*. Beverly Hills, Calif: Sage. **11**.

Patton, M. Q. (1981) *Creative Evaluation*. Newbury Park, Calif: Sage. **45**.

Patton, M. Q. (1982) *Practical Evaluation*. Newbury Park, Calif: Sage. **15, 19, 45, 92**.

Patton, M. Q. (1990) *Qualitative Evaluation and Research Methods*. Newbury Park, Calif: Sage. **98**.

Patton, M. Q. (1994) Developmental evaluation. *Evaluation Practice*, 15, 311–20. **50**.

Pawson, R. and Tilley, N. (1997) *Realistic Evaluation*. London: Sage. **55, 69, 71, 73, 74, 118**.

Pawson, R. and Tilley, N. (1998) Workshop on applying scientific realism to evaluative practice. Kirklees Education Welfare Service, Cliffe House, Shepley, March. **74**.

Percy-Smith, J. (ed.) (1996) *Needs Assessment in Public Policy*. Milton Keynes: Open University Press. **127, 134**.

Pettigrew, T. F. (1996) *How to Think Like a Social Scientist*. New York: HarperCollins. **53**.

Pole, C. (1993) Local and national evaluation. In R. G. Burgess (ed.) *Educational Research and Evaluation: For Policy and Practice?* London: Falmer. **67**.

Porteous, D. (1996) Methodologies for needs assessment. In J. Percy-Smith (ed.). *Needs Assessment in Public Policy*. Milton Keynes: Open University Press. **133**.

Posovac, E. J. and Carey, R. G. (1997) *Program Evaluation: Methods and Case Studies*. 5th Edn.

Upper Saddle River, NJ: Prentice-Hall. **49, 52, 72, 96.**

Renzetti, C. M. and Lee, R. M. (eds.) (1993) *Researching Sensitive Topics.* Newbury Park, Calif: Sage. **40.**

Repper, J. and Perkins, R. (1998) Assessing the needs of people who are disabled by serious ongoing mental health problems. In S. Baldwin (ed.). *Needs Assessment in Community Care: Clinical Practice and Policy Making.* Oxford: Butterworth-Heinemann. **131, 134.**

Robson, C. (1993) *Real World Research: A Resource for Social Scientists and Practitioner-Researchers.* Oxford: Blackwell. **21, 61, 82, 98.**

Robson, C. (1994) *Experiment, Design and Statistics in Psychology.* 3rd Edn. Harmondsworth: Penguin. **57, 115.**

Rossi, P. H. and Freeman, H. E. (1993) *Evaluation: A Systematic Approach.* 5th Edn. Newbury Park, Calif: Sage. **11, 43, 66.**

Sanday, A. (1993) The relationship between educational research and evaluation and the role of the local education authority. In R. G. Burgess (ed.) *Educational Research and Evaluation: For Policy and Practice?* London: Falmer. **42.**

Sayer, A. (1992) *Method in Social Science: A Realist Approach.* 2nd Edn. London: Routledge. **71.**

Schon, D. A. (1983) *The Reflective Practitioner.* London: Temple Smith. **24.**

Schon, D. A. (1987) *Educating the Reflective Practitioner.* San Francisco: Jossey-Bass. **24.**

Scriven, M. (1967) The methodology of evaluation. *AERA Monograph Series in Curriculum Evaluation,* 1, 39–83. **50.**

Scriven, M. (1991) *Evaluation Thesaurus.* 4th Edn. Newbury Park, Calif: Sage. **69.**

Seidman, E. and Rappoport, J. (eds.) (1986) *Redefining Social Problems.* New York: Plenum. **128.**

Selener, D. (1997) *Participatory Action Research and Social Change. Cornell Participatory Action Research Network.* Ithaca, NY: Cornell University. **7.**

Shadish, W. R., Cook, T. D. and Leviton, L. C. (1991) *Foundations of Program Evaluation: Theories of Practice.* Newbury Park, Calif: Sage. **11.**

Sheldon, B. (1983) The use of single case experimental designs in the evaluation of social work. *British Journal of Social Work,* 13, 477–500. **61.**

Sheldon, B. (1986) Social work effectiveness experiments: review and implications. *British Journal of Social Work,* 16, 223–42. **57.**

Sidman, M. (1960) *The Tactics of Scientific Research.* New York: Basic Books. **60.**

Sieber, J. E. (1992) *Planning Ethically Responsible Research: A Guide for Students and Internal Review Boards.* Newbury Park, Calif: Sage. **31, 39, 40.**

Sieber, J. E. (1998) Planning ethically responsible research. In L. Bickman and D. J. Rog (eds.). *Handbook of Applied Social Research Methods.* Thousand Oaks, Calif: Sage. **31, 33, 37.**

Stewart, D. W. and Shamdasani, P. N. (1998) Focus group research: exploration and discovery. In L. Bickman and D. J. Rog (eds.). *Handbook of Applied Social Research Methods.* Thousand Oaks, Calif: Sage. **93, 94.**

Strauss, A. I. and Corbin, J. (1999) *Basics of Qualitative Research: Techniques and Procedures for Developing Grounded Theory.* 2nd Edn. Thousand Oaks, Calif: Sage. **119.**

Thyer, B. A. (1993) Single-system research designs. In R. M. Grinnell (ed.) *Social Work Research and Evaluation* 4th Edn. Itasca, Ill: F. E. Peacock. **60.**

Tufte, E. R. (1983) *The Visual Display of Quantitative Information.* Cheshire, Conn: Graphics Press. **121.**

Tyler, R. (1991) General statement on program evaluation. In M. W. McLaughlin and D. C. Phillips (eds.) *Ninetieth Yearbook of the National Society for the Study of Education. Part 2* (original work published in *Journal of Education Resources,* 1942). Chicago: NSSE and University of Chicago Press. **62.**

Webb, E. J., Campbell, D. T., Schwartz, R. D., Sechrest, L. and Grove, J. B. (1981) *Nonreactive Measures in the Social Sciences.* 2nd Edn. Boston Mass: Houghton Mifflin. **97.**

Weiler, D. (1976) A public school voucher demonstration: the first year of Alum Rock, summary and conclusions. In G. V. Glass (ed.) *Evaluation Studies Review Annual* (Vol. 1).

Beverly Hills, Calif: Sage. **43**.

Weiss, C. H. (1972) *Evaluation Research: Methods for Assessing Program Effectiveness*. London: Prentice-Hall. **71**.

Weiss, C. H. (1987) The circuitry of enlightenment. *Knowledge: Creation, Diffusion, Utilisation*, 8, 274–81. **11**.

Weiss, C. H. (1989) Congressional committees as users of analysis. *Journal of Policy Analysis and Management*, 8, 411–31. **125**.

Weiss, C. H. (1995) Nothing so practical as a good theory: exploring theory-based evaluation for comprehensive community inititives for children and families. In J. P. Connell, A. C. Kubisch, L. B. Schorr and C. H. Weiss (eds.) *New Approaches to Evaluating Community Initiatives*. Washington, DC: Aspen Institute. **70**.

Weiss, C. H. (1997) How can theory-based evaluation make greater headway? *Evaluation Review*, 21, 501–24. **70**.

Weiss, C. H. (1998) *Evaluation: Methods for Studying Programs and Policies*. 2nd Edn. Upper Saddle River, NJ: Prentice-Hall. **51, 64, 71, 75, 125**.

Weitzman, E. A. and Miles, M. B. (1995) *Computer Programs for Qualitative Data Analysis: A Software Sourcebook*. Thousand Oaks, Calif: Sage. **119**.

Yates, B. T. (1996) *Analysing Costs, Procedures, Processes, and Outcomes in Human Services*. Thousand Oaks, Calif: Sage. **138, 139**.

Yates, B. T. (1998) Formative evaluation of costs, cost-effectiveness, and cost-benefit: toward cost → procedure → process → outcome analysis. In L. Bickman and D. J. Rog (eds.). *Handbook of Applied Social Research Methods*. Thousand Oaks, Calif: Sage. **136**.

INDEX